STUDENT OF A MASTER

HOWARD F GIBBON

LAMPADA PRESS

LAMPADA PRESS
Cottingham Road
Hull
HU6 7RX

A CIP catalogue record for this book is available from the British Library.

© **Howard Gibbon**

Published 1997

Paperback ISBN 1 873811 04 7

Printed by
Advanced Laser Press
Digital Park
Longstanton
Cambridge

STUDENT OF A MASTER

HOWARD F GIBBON

Acknowledgments

I would like to thank my students, past and present, for their support over the years as I have striven to pass on the teaching of the Taoist arts of T'ai Chi and Feng Shou as taught to me by my Master Chee Soo.

Many times my path has crossed with others due to the medium of the Taoist arts. Sometimes the strange twists and turns of life separated us as our paths took different directions, but without fail I learned from each and every one of them, and for this I am deeply grateful. I hope that they in turn benefited from their association with me.

I am particularly grateful to Dr. Bruce Woodcock, whom some fifteen years ago sowed the seed in my head during a class when he suggested that I write this book. Likewise I would like to thank the author Domini Highsmith, a student of mine, her advice and friendship has been invaluable. The confidence of these two people coupled with the love of my two children, Tracey and Leanne gave me the courage to complete the task.

Before this book was complete I met my partner, Gisela. Her encouragement and assistance in the editing of my manuscript have been invaluable in the preparation of this work. I express my thanks and gratitude to you Gisela. At this point I would like to mention Gisela's son Taio, for no other reason than he trains hard and is turning into a fine young man.

To my departed master, Chee Soo, to whom I owe a great debt, which I can only attempt to repay by carrying on the work he bestowed upon me. The work that I was obliged to accept, for after being given so much how could I refuse to share it with others. There are no words that can express the depth of my gratitude to this man who was my mentor for so many years. The only words that seem fitting are simply *"Thanks for the training, master"*.

CONTENTS

Introduction

The weather was rather cold with a strong breeze, making the air feel fresh and invigorating as I was out walking one lovely day late in March 1990. I felt a sense of urgency. I had been tentatively thinking for sometime now that I should write a book about my understanding of the Taoists Arts of T'ai chi, self defence and the philosophy out of which these arts were born. It was my great honour and privilege for 21 years to be a student of Master Chee Soo. During my first 10 years of study I read many books on T'ai Chi and self defence; during the last ten years I have grown more and more interested in the philosophy behind these arts. This has led me to study many books on Eastern Philosophy, particularly on Taoist thought. Many of these books are written by academics who merely translate the Chinese text into English. Since they do not follow the way themselves they lose much of the essence of the original teaching and often degenerate into intellectual argument over various points.

I feel that as there is a great interest in T'ai Chi and Eastern Philosophy at the present time that a book written by one who is aspiring to follow the Tao of his own life, one who has trained under a Taoist Master for 21 years and is also a westerner by birth, may be able to make a contribution in some way.

I have learnt to see the world through different eyes. It is the same world in constant movement, conforming to the laws of nature (Tao). It has not changed, but my outlook has, and I would not wish to return to my former self. Nor could anything repay my master for what he has done for me.

I know from experience that the hardest part of any task is the first bit, and once you have actually started, the task does not seem so impossible any more. As it says in an old Chinese proverb: A thousand mile journey starts with a single step.

And so later on in this lovely spring day I began a new episode in my life. As I put pen to paper I felt at the same time excitement, humility and unworthiness at the task that lay before me. This brought to mind a quote from Thomas A Edison, which I have framed and hung on the wall in my living room as a constant reminder to be more courageous in the way I live my life. There was only me to hear, but I read it out loud all the same.

IF WE DID ALL WE ARE CAPABLE OF DOING

WE WOULD LITERALLY ASTONISH OURSELVES.

Knowledge is all around us, not just in books. Many things can be learnt from books, but true knowledge must come by direct experience. I have had the unique opportunity to train with an individual who devoted his life to learning and teaching the Taoist Arts.

Sadly, my master died in August 1994 before this book was published. Although I discussed it with him he never read the manuscript before he passed on. Some parts of the book are written in the present tense, but, I have decided to leave the text unaltered so it will express my thoughts and feelings as they were at the time they were written. For a while after Chee Soo's passing I lost interest in the publication of this book as I dealt with my grief. Without my mentor to guide me and chide me I felt lost and confused. Then, slowly, with the passage of a little time, came the realization that my adolescence in the arts had ended and it was time to embrace life on my own. I had the seeds of understanding passed on to me by a unique master. I made the choice to renew my efforts to publish this book and carry on the work my master undertook. For what use is knowledge unless it is put to a purpose?

Once I made the choice to take action things started to fall into place. But choice is the wrong word really, it is an obligation. For after being given so much how could I be so selfish as to refuse to share it with others? So, another lesson for me. There was no choice at all; it was an illusion, there was only a compliance with my predestined path, a willingness to move with the flow into uncharted waters, a willingness to embrace the fears and not hide from them, the realization that I am poorly prepared, but the knowledge that wisdom comes from the living of life. The mistakes I will surely make are the stepping stones to my success - the courage to step into the arena of life and endure the Yin phases that come my way and rejoice in the Yang phases, the excitement of the contest of life that fills me with a glorious happiness and enriches my life. Sometimes I get battered by life and I come out sweating, dusty and bruised, but the joy of triumph over adversity is preferable to me to the dull existence of those who never suffer defeat or experience the exhilaration of success because they never do anything that has an element of risk, preferring to do nothing so they can never be proved wrong. So, if you like the journey, revel in the struggle, and then unashamedly enjoy the rewards, you will find much to interest you in these pages.

YIN AND YANG

The two opposing yet complimentary forces of yin and yang are the underlying factors behind Chinese thought. They are inherent in Chinese philosophy and medicine, and are depicted by many works of art, indeed they are at the root of Chinese culture.

In my experience most Westerners, when introduced to the principles of yin and yang see them only as opposing forces, bad or good, negative and positive, and they classify them accordingly. Let us take a few examples and try to see how these two fundamental principles not only oppose, but also compliment each other. Yin encompasses moon, night, darkness, water, cold, female, contraction. Yang encompasses sun, day, light, fire, heat, male, expansion. First we must understand that nothing is totally yin or yang, each has a little of the other present in varying degrees. This can be seen by examining the above yin and yang characteristics. The moon appears at night when it is dark. Night, dark and moon are yin, but the moon which waxes and wanes depending on the time of the month, gives us and the rest of the animal kingdom a little light with which to see by, which is yang. The sun, which is yang, gives us warmth and light, without which plants would not grow and there would be no food to sustain life. When the sun is at its peak animals seek the shade, which is yin, and we humans, if we venture out at this time, need to drink more fluids, which are yin, to keep our body temperature normal. If the sun shone continuously all plant life would shrivel up and die, the rivers and sea would eventually dry up and all life would cease, for all life needs water to survive. So permanent yang is not good. If the Earth were perpetually in darkness, plants would not grow and there would be no food to feed the animal kingdom. So permanent yin is not good. So while it is true that Yin and yang are opposites, they also harmonise, for without either life as we know it could not exist on our planet. Without either male or female human life could not continue. While man and women have, since the beginning of life on earth, had difficulty understanding one another, they must co-operate and harmonise with each other to continue the species.

Have you noticed how women are taking more prominent roles in society? Many of the top jobs in financial and other institutions are now held by women. Many women are entering politics. We have had our first woman Prime Minister. Employers suffer increasingly from a shortage of skilled labour and they are encouraging women to return to work. Many women who left the workforce to start a family already have the skills required which may only need updating in line with modern techniques. All yin things eventually become yang and yang becomes yin. Night becomes day and day becomes night. Man has ruled since he first roamed the earth. Slowly, woman is becoming the dominant partner. Of course, this process will take many hundreds of years to complete, but the evidence is there for anyone willing to look. More and more men are taking time off work to look after the children while the woman continues to work, and modern man helps more with the domestic chores which would have been frowned on by yesterday's macho man. However, not all men and women follow this pattern, it merely shows a general trend. As all yin and yang things contain a little of the other. So all yin and yang conditions contain a little of the other, and the potential to change to its opposite.

Too much pleasure will turn to pain. If you have a night out on the town over-indulging in food and drink you will surely suffer for it the following day. And if you continue to do this on a regular basis your health will inevitably deteriorate. Strike a balance in all things: the food we eat, work and rest, spending time with others and finding time for yourselves.

Balance in all these is essential to our well being, But we are all individuals and what suits one does not necessarily suit another. We must each find our own balance, no one else can do it for us. It is just like learning to ride a bicycle. People can show you how to turn the pedals to provide motion, move the handlebars to change direction and apply the brakes to stop. The only thing they cannot teach you is how to keep your balance on the bike, you just have to get on and keep falling off until you master it. You must suffer the humiliating laughter of other people as you continuously fail to keep your balance on the bike; failure in the eyes of others that is, as failure is only a stepping stone to success. If you wish to learn to keep your balance you must be resolute in the face of such humiliation and be determined in your efforts because no other human being can show you how, you must do it for yourself.

It is not that Yang is good and yin bad, as is often thought. Yin is the opposing yet complimentary force to yang. All perfectly natural. It is the darkness that makes the light useful. A little story may help to illustrate this point. A man lived with his wife on a small farm in the hills from which they barely managed to grow enough food with which to feed themselves. The man's wife became pregnant and the people from neighbouring farms came to congratulate them, saying "It is good that you will have a child."

He said, "Why do you say it is good?"

When the child was born it was a boy, but sadly the woman died giving birth. The neighbours came round to pay their respects when he buried his wife. They said how sad for him to have lost his wife and to have the added burden of bringing up the child by himself. "It is just too bad," they said.

He said, "Why do you say it is bad?"

One day a big black stallion wandered on to his farm. The man caught it and used it to help him till the fields. His neighbours said of his good fortune. "It is good that you have a horse to help you till the fields." He said, "Why do you say it is good?"

One night the stallion jumped the fence and ran off. The neighbours said, "What a shame, it is too bad". The man said, "Why do you say it is bad?"

A short while later the stallion returned with a herd of horses.

His neighbours said, "How fortunate, that's good."

The man said, "Why do you say it is good?"

The boy was out riding the stallion one day when he fell off and broke his leg. It set badly and he walked with a limp. His neighbours said, "It is just too bad."

He said, "Why do you say it is bad?"

War broke out in the country and all the young men were called to arms. But because of his limp the man's son did not have to go. His neighbours said, "It is good your son does not have to go to war where he may get killed and leave you all alone."

The man said, "Why do you say it is good?"

The following winter the son caught a chest infection and died. He had not been very strong since his accident and suffered many minor ills. The neighbours came to pay their respects when the man buried his son.

They said, "It's too bad you are now an old man and all alone.

The man said, "Why do you say it is bad?"

Every thing has its yin and yang aspect, although we can usually only see one side. We tend to focus on either the yin or yang aspect, depending on the situation and conditions at the time. We label things good or bad because they are coloured by our own personnel desires and what we want to happen. One should learn to look at the other side of the situation, so one can get a true understanding of what is really happening. In other words, learn to see things as they really are. I will explain in the chapter on T'ai Chi how the practice of this art slowly brings the student to an awareness of first their own reality, how they can learn to see themselves as they are, now, not coloured by the past or their expectations of the future. Then we can start to appreciate that in spite of all the problems in the world it is a truly beautiful place. However, before we can do that we must start at the beginning. We must understand and appreciate ourselves first, and see the part we play within our society. Our own personal contribution to society, no matter how humble, has great value. If you work as a cleaning lady or a dustman, you provide a valuable service to the community. Without someone performing these tasks the cities, inside and outside, would soon become horrible places, smelly and rodent infested. Have you noticed there are no salesmen any more only consultants and advisors, fewer secretaries, and more personal assistants to managing directors? A fancy name only makes you more important in your own eyes. The way you perform your work is what ultimately people, and the Tao (god), notice. If you are a dustman (sorry, refuse disposal technician) and if you do your work cheerfully, conscientiously and with dignity, you may be financially and materially, small and humble, but you offer a giant service to your fellow man.

Woman is attracted to man; man is attracted to woman. If the positive pole of a magnet is placed in close proximity to the negative pole of another magnet they are attracted to each other. Or should I say they are attracted by each other? It does not really matter, does it? The important thing is that they are attracted towards each other. Place two positive magnetic poles close to each other and they repel one another. Have you noticed how boys, and men, have a tendency to compete with each other? Nearly all their leisure activities involve direct competition. All these things are perfectly natural conforming to the natural order of the Tao. If we send a man into space, he must eventually return to earth his natural habitat to replenish his air and food supplies or perish. If we send a man deep into the ocean or deep beneath the earth's crust the same applies because the surface of the earth is the place where all we need to exist occurs naturally, food, water and air. I am not suggesting that science should not explore these regions. On the contrary, I believe that knowledge of the material world and beyond does not disprove the principle of yin and yang, but enhances our understanding of these composite factors of all phenomena in the universe and merely confirms their validity.

Let us consider a fairly recent innovation in technology. We are now firmly in the age of the computer. Incidentally, before the electronic device we now call a computer was invented, a computer was the name given to a person who made calculations. And who invented the first mechanical means of computing? The Chinese. They invented the Abacus, an oblong frame with rows of wires or groves along which beads slide. Anyway back to the computers and the yin and yang, before I drift off the subject. Now the basic language that a computer understands is called machine language and it is represented by a number system called binary which consists of a (1) which represents positive and a (0) which represents negative. In electronic terms these are represented by an on switch (1) and an off switch (0). All the high level languages that programmers use such, as basic, cobol, pascal, etc. are converted into this binary number system. The reason for programmers using high level languages to programme in instead of machine language is that the human brain finds it extremely difficult to deal with all those ones and zeros. So all the graphics, mathematical calculation, desktop publishing and word processing done on a computer is ultimately converted into machine language, that is, binary, which is the only language the computer actually understands. And this computer which is capable of producing an astonishing variety of manifestations can only differentiate between a one or a zero, or more precisely between an on or an off state in a tiny transistor. Furthermore, the computer must have a power source before it can be used.This power source is at present electricity. Perhaps sometime in the future we will have solar powered computers.

All living things must have a power source to exist on earth in the state we term living. In the East, various names are given to this mysterious power source. It need not concern us what its name is;we only need to understand that without it life on earth ceases. The analogy between sentient life and modern day's greatest invention, the computer, is that in order to be able to function they both need to be given a source of power, and they both require the opposing yet harmonious principles of yin and yang or positive and negative. In the sentient world we have a power source (spirit, if you prefer), yin and yang and from these the Tao (god) manifested the myriad creatures. In the phenomenal world of the computer we have a power source (electricity), positive (1) and negative (0) and from these modern technology is developing a myriad of uses that are greatly enhancing human existence. However, there is potential for good and bad in this modern invention. Who could fail to notice the increase in advertising literature pouring though their letter-boxes since its use became prolific, encouraging people to buy more and more? As with everything in our world, the sentient and materialistic, we need to constantly seek to balance the yin and yang aspect. And so it is with this wonderful modern invention. We must make stringent efforts to balance the computer's potential for good and bad. So it can be put to good use to serve mankind and not become our master. In the wrong hands the computer has the potential to become an enormous monster, limiting man's freedom and erasing his dignity. It is important that we tend our world like a good gardener tends his garden. His love of life and his love of God are shown in the way he encourages growth. When he plants a new seed he clears the weeds to make sure the seed can establish its roots. He sees it has plenty of water until the roots develop, and once it has grown into a beautiful flower he constantly keeps an eye on the weeds to make sure they do not overrun the garden and choke the flowers and plants. He takes care of all the flowers in the garden, not just the one he planted, for each flower is unique and beautiful in its own right, but the garden consists of all the flowers. He tends them all with equal care. However, recently we have seen great strides towards improving the environment and the quality of life, and I have faith that this will continue. We should not fear the future as no doubt the world is unfolding as it should.

Science has shown us that matter cannot be destroyed, we can only change its state. We can boil water long enough and it becomes steam; make it cold enough and it becomes ice. When we heat water we make it more yang and we can use this to make a warming drink on a cold day. We can use ice to keep our drinks cool on a hot day. Care should be taken not to be too extreme, however. As we discussed earlier, too yang or too yin can be catastrophic. For instance a drink that is too hot will burn your mouth and a drink that is too cold will chill your insides, neither of which is conducive to good health.

We should also be aware that sometimes we have to balance the yin and yang aspects of a situation or condition and make a choice. We can take the invention of the wheel which has been around long enough now to be accepted into our daily lives to such an extent that we consider it a necessity and give it very little thought. The wheel has given us great benefits.We can move goods more easily from one place to another; we can visit places by bus, train or car which were hitherto out of reach to us; our lives are enriched by this movement of goods and people. We are able to enjoy many new experiences. All this and more is now available to us because of the invention of the wheel. That is the yang side. The yin side is, large areas of our countryside have been taken and replaced by a network of roads. As traffic builds up new roads are laid to reduce the congestion. Many people, travel in vehicles to places they had no need to go to in the past. A large part of many people's working time is spent sitting in a vehicle travelling from one place to the next. In London the traffic is so bad that it moves on average slower than in the days of the horse and carriage. So people sit in their expensive cars capable of high speeds, crawling along the roads of London in the rush hour belching out pollution into the atmosphere. Still, when something becomes too yin it will start to turn yang again. This is the natural law of the Universe of which the yin and yang are an infinite principle. I do not know how this problem will eventually be solved, but I know it will because.It must be, otherwise the traffic will get so bad people will either not get enough sleep through having to set off so early for work that they will be (if they are not already) inefficient at work though lack of proper sleep. Or the working day will be reduced by the travelling time involved in getting to work. On top of this, hundreds of thousands of people are injured on our roads every year, many of them losing their lives. To give up the wheel and all its benefits would throw our world into turmoil. There is not any-one in this country that would not be affected.It would reduce the quality of life of every man, woman and child. I wonder how many people would be prepared to return to a world without the wheel? This may seem to you to be an unfair question. Is it an unfair question or is it that you prefer not to face reality? All these problems, injuries and deaths are real and they are a result of the use of the wheel. Of course the wheel is not really to blame but the person controlling it. If we drove our cars like a good gardener tends his garden there would be fewer accidents on the road. It may be impractical to remove the wheel from our world, but we should be aware of our responsibilities to our fellow man and our environment as we use it. I am sure the inventors of the wheel had no idea of the catastrophes that would result from their invention. However, it is like the rose in our garden; if we accept the beauty of its flower we must also accept the thorns on its stem. And when we, as all those who tend them occasionally do, prick ourselves on those thorns, let it serve to remind us that we must care for our gardens and our world with the same love and devotion. Then the world will become a beautiful place, at least for those who care and serve mankind. We must do our best at work and play in the knowledge that we will sometimes make mistakes. You cannot hide away from life for fear of making mistakes. Life is for living; it is a beautiful world; we will constantly experience good times (yang) and bad times (yin), but they are never all good or bad.In fact, good and bad really do not exist, there is only life with its opposing yet harmonious principles balancing one thing with another. Our knowledge of this interaction will always be partial. Full understanding is beyond our comprehension.

An ant carries a load that looks incredibly heavy for such a small creature and struggles on with its heavy load, seeking its way back to the nest, working for the good of its community. Ants are amazingly hard working creatures who have developed an order and discipline within their community that is enviable. They have developed a structure to their society that enables them to survive and prosper in many parts of the world that are inhospitable. They work together in harmony, each doing its own task and contributing to the survival of the species. Now, do those ants comprehend the world as we do? No. They are limited in their understanding of the phenomenal world compared to us humans. But they have a structure to their society that provides food and care for its members and enables them to survive as a community. I would like to share a lesson I received one day at school when I was nine years old. One morning our English teacher came into the classroom and wrote this on the blackboard.

Ds r ⚡ ds r r d d r d l d r d r o l I.

He asked us if anyone could read it to him. We thought for awhile, But none of us could decipher its meaning. He smiled and underneath wrote.

"These are ants these are".

"Are they"?

"They are".

"The Hell they are".

"They are"!

"Oh! Hell I"

He then went on to explain that without a basic understanding of spelling, punctuation etc, communication using the written word was extremely difficult and as in the above example virtually impossible. We cannot all be writers, newspaper reporters or English teachers, but we can all learn to read and write so that we can communicate with each other, and be more effective members of society. The yin aspect of learning can be quite stressful, but it is more than compensated for by the yang aspect of being able to communicate with others effectively, even if that is only by being able to write to a loved one who is temporarily elsewhere. Like the ants, we must have discipline and order. We must learn to work together for the good of the human race as a whole. Like the gardener and the ant, we must look after our world as best we can, so we too can survive. We must each do our bit, no matter how humble, to serve mankind, with as much love and care as we can muster. Then, perhaps, we will one day live in harmony with all God's creatures and the environment as opposed to against it, endeavouring to balance the yin and yang of our own lives with that of nature, like the ants who do not comprehend our world. Our knowledge too is limited. God created our world, and by studying nature we can learn much about the reality of our own lives.

Finally, it must be remembered that all things are in constant movement, nothing is stationary. We stand or sit still, but our heart is still beating, our blood still courses through our veins and we are on a world that is constantly revolving. We perceive a table as a solid object, yet science has proved that the molecules that form the wood are vibrating constantly. Those molecules, along with those in other apparently solid objects, merely vibrate on a scale so slow as to appear - to our naked eye that is - motionless.

The condition of wood left open to air and moisture eventually deteriorates, so we paint or varnish the wood to protect it. Then the paint deteriorates, so we scrape it off, rub down the wood and put fresh paint on. Eventually we have to replace the wood, but we have slowed down the process of deterioration. Why do we do this? In the past our ancestors did not bother to paint tables, chairs, window frames or other wooden objects. When a chair or table became unserviceable they simply cut down a tree and made another one. However, the population was smaller then and there was an abundance of trees everywhere. Today things are different. The population has increased; more chairs and tables are needed than ever before. Wood by comparison is in short supply and has become expensive. Wood also takes a long time to grow and we are quickly learning that if we use it faster than it grows we are upsetting the balance of nature. Wood is not only useful to make things with. Much of our wildlife depends on the tree for its food, shelter and its environment. A single oak tree can feed and be a home for many hundreds of other species. An average of 284 insects live on oak trees. Some feed on the flowers and leaves and others eat the bark. The insects attract birds. The acorns are eaten by both birds and mammals. This attracts predators like the sparrowhawk and weasel. Trees are the longest-living organisms on earth. As well as being beautiful and majestic they perform a service to us and improve the quality of our lives.

Trees recycle nutrients to and from the soil. By stabilizing the soil they reduce erosion by wind and water. They modify climatic extremes by affecting air flow, temperature and humidity. And perhaps the most important of all the tree's gifts to us is its process of photosynthesis which is essential to life on earth. Trees use the energy of sunlight to convert atmospheric CO_2 and water into oxygen. Trees also trap particles of dust, smoke and fumes on their leaves, branches and stems. This is then washed to the ground by the next fall of rain. 2.5 acres of beech wood are able to extract about 4 tons of dust per year from the atmosphere, cleaning the air for us. Acting as a humidifier a single beech tree transpires 75 - 100 gallons of water on a summer's day, cooling and refreshing the air. Tree felling in the Alps and the Himalayas produced landslides and floods. Excessive tree felling also exacerbated the famine in Africa by causing soil erosion when it rained and encouraged the encroachment of the dessert. Hedgerows, thousands of miles of which were torn up after the war, are Britain's richest wildlife reserves. The hedgerow also has a practical use, it can slow down wind speeds for up to 10 times its height, reducing soil erosion and increasing crop yields. We humans, if we are foolish enough to cut down too many trees, not only commit other species to extinction, but reduce the quality of our own lives in the process. We pollute the air with our cars and factories, then cut down the trees which help clean the air and provide us with oxygen. We need to pay as much attention to our future supply of air as we do to nuclear disarmament. New materials have had to be found to make the chairs and tables, but more needs to be done, for we are cutting down the rain forest at an alarming rate, which will provide short term gain for some and long term misery for others. We can help by teaching our children to respect wildlife and the environment because our children are the future custodians of our planet. They must be educated so they balance future technological advancement with nature. If we destroy the balance of nature we will destroy ourselves in the process.

All things and all phenomena in the universe, on our planet and within ourselves, are constantly changing their yin and yang influence. Every thing is constantly moving and changing, never static or stationary. Nothing is completely yin or yang. Everything is relative, one with the other. Each harmonises with the other to maintain the balance.

God gave us the gift of life and the bounty of the earth on which to live it. Let us take care of it like the precious jewel that it is.

The Tao

Taoism is a mystery to most westerners. 'The Tao', usually translated as 'The Way', is thought by many to be a way of life. Others
believe Taoism comes from the occult. Some people think Taoism
is an Eastern form of religion.

Taoism has much to offer to modern man. It is just as relevant to
today's society as it was when it was formulated in ancient China,
for the truth shines through. In fact I believe that we desperately
need to return to the values available to us through the practice
and understanding of Taoist philosophy. People are beginning to
look to the East for answers to questions they are formulating
themselves about the meaning of life and the part they play in it.
In the East they have for thousands of years been deeply investigating
the nature of man and his place in the cosmos, whereas in the
West we have been largely more concerned with improving the
material side of life, improving man's everyday conditions to make
the physical side of life more comfortable. So, whilst in the East
they concentrated on the internal, we on the other hand concentrated
on the external. I point this out, not to say one is right and the
other wrong, but just to make a note of the point that this is the
way things are. It is another example of the Yin and Yang.

The interesting thing is that whilst many people in the West now
seek the esoteric knowledge of the East, the East now seeks to
learn and make use of our discoveries. Through this sharing of
knowledge, the potential for harmony between nations has never
been greater. But, just as there is a little Yin in all Yang things and
a little Yang in all Yin things, during this time of harmony when
nations come closer together, we have to be aware of the possibility

of disharmony due to cultural differences, and the differences in thinking patterns. But with open minds and open hearts these differences can be resolved. The study of the 'Tao Te Ching', the Chinese classical work written by Lao Tzu, will be of great benefit to all those who seek to improve the way they deal with both everyday life, conditions at work, personal relationships and spiritual values. It has been translated many times by scholars, in fact the only other book that has been translated more often is the Bible. As mentioned above, the Tao is often described as 'The Way'. I feel this is the most apt description. The Tao, thought of in this context, can be many things, the way of nature, the way of the world, the way (path) of one's own life. The wisdom offered through the study of Taoist philosophy is applicable to each of these. Like the eminent scientists of today who study the theory of Chaos, those ancient Chinese scholars learnt that everything in the universe is in perpetual movement and that everything effects everything else. If there is a movement somewhere it effects something somewhere else. The exponents of Chaos theory explain this by the example that if a butterfly were to flap its wings at the edge of the universe this action might create a tornado somewhere on our planet. And so it is that the scientists of the West and the mystics of the East are coming to realize that these two apparently opposite doctrines are one. Like the Yin and Yang they are the two composite factors that account for all our experiences, physical and spiritual, each separate in its own right yet part of the whole.

Those who scorn Taoism as being part of the occult, who think that Taoists spend their time indulging in magical practices, have not met a sincere follower of 'The Way'. There is NOTHING magical about Taoism.Everything, including Chi and Li energies, is completely natural and available to anyone.

However, if by occult the meaning is mystical in the sense of contemplation and self-surrender to obtain an understanding of the ultimate reality (Tao), then I would agree that Taoism has an occult element. The spiritual truths obtained through contemplating the Tao, whilst always beyond intellectual understanding, and always limited, can be known. If one can learn to see clearly with the eyes and listen clearly with the ears, unfettered by one's individual desires and ambition, one can learn the truth. And whilst this knowledge one has gained is always only partial one knows what one knows!

As a student of the Taoist arts I have always felt the training and study to be like climbing up the stairs of a multi-story building. Climbing the stairs, round and upwards, the steps look identical, and when one reaches the first floor the steps to the second floor appear the same. Up we climb to the third floor. Again, the steps along the way look the same. We appear to have gone nowhere because the path before us looks identical. We have raised ourselves up a level or two. But we do not indulge in self praise. The journey ahead is long and arduous and we cannot afford to waste precious energy in illusions of self-importance. We do not look back, for we do not wish to return, our only thoughts are of the journey ahead. Fo,r from the very first day we came upon the door to the building, we knew instinctively that this was the right path for us. Without even understanding where the destination would lead us, we fearfully stepped through the door and tentatively began the climb. Others turn back at the door, afraid to enter the unknown. That is their choice. They will be brought to the door again and again until they are ready to make the journey. They are not forced to start on the journey. We are all given choices at various times in our lives and have to make decisions. There are no right or wrong decisions either really, because once we choose one path we exclude the other choices and alter forever the conditions that surround us. The choice we make affects us and those around us, and we will learn according to these conditions. We cannot return to the original point and change our choice, because the past is irretrievable. We can of course make new choices in the light of lessons learnt.

So there is no point in indulging in self pity or bitterness, thinking that if you or someone else had done things differently things would be better. It is much better to use your energies in a positive way to deal with things as they are. For this is your reality, right now. If you wallow in self pity or bitterness with your mind steeped in the past, or dream of a glorious life were everyone is happy and content sometime in the future, you lose contact with the present and therefore with reality. You enter the world of illusions and cease to be aware of the present. The Tao has arranged things as they are so that certain lessons can be learnt, and if we allow ourselves to drift excessively into the past or the future we blind ourselves to the present and restrict our own development.

The Taoist tries to surrender his self, so that his decisions are not influenced by his individual desire and ambitions. His decisions are made for him, unfettered by matters of the world. This makes him seem rather strange to others because the Taoist does not follow the structured patterns that are born out of logical reasoning of the intellect, as do most people. The Taoist however, once he has reached this level of understanding of the working of the Tao, has no fear, because whilst he still suffers from the ways of the world, and is still sometimes adversely affected by the desires of his fellow man, he remains entire and untouched by these accepting them, as he accepts that night must follow day. He is aware of the awe-inspiring beauty around us, nature, people and the interactive movement between them, which is the Tao. Seeing this at work each day enables the Taoist to enjoy a serenity and happiness that is beyond the comprehension of those steeped in their own desires, ambition and greed.

Taoism has been depicted as a religion many times in the past and some people who study the subject believe that Taoism is a replacement for - what shall we say? - orthodox religion. I consider this incorrect. Religion is generally expressed as belief in God, who is a superhuman being controlling everything in the universe and entitled to obedience and worship. As a student of a remarkable Taoist Master, my studies have shown me that Taoism does not conform to this definition. So, whilst I am a practising Taoist, I also consider myself a Christian, and I say my prayers each morning and each evening. For me there is no conflict between the two. When I say my prayers I do not picture a benign white bearded old man to represent God. To me God is a universal spirit, omnipresent, and therefore he can be with us any time we ask and we can speak to him any time we wish and he will always hear us. He is always there for us, but we are not always there for him.

Sometimes we get confused and think he has deserted us. He has not. WE have excluded him. Through my prayer and meditations I feel I have a direct telephone line to God; IF ONLY I COULD STOP TALKING SO MUCH AND JUST LISTEN MORE.

The Tao is the way of things, the natural order that permeates the chaos that surrounds us. It cannot be analysed by the intellect because in the time it takes to complete the analysis things are no longer as they were. Everything in the universe is constantly moving and that movement affects everything else. Complete chaos in fact. But not to the supreme spirit (God). So here we have a meeting point between God and the Tao, One as the omnipresent supreme spirit giving order to the chaos of the universe, and the Tao as the way things are, the natural order of things.

To me the Tao and God are the same thing and both are beyond my understanding. Yet whilst being the same they are somehow separate, just as the Yin and Yang aspects are separate yet part of the same thing, the darkness of night and the light of day, separate and different yet part of the cycle we use to regulate our time and give order to our lives.

So how does one learn to understand these things? Well you must find your own way, but I will tell you my methods of attaining knowledge. I pray and ask for understanding because somewhere in the Bible it is written 'Ask and it shall be given'. Asking alone is not enough though, the INTENTION must be correct. I try to understand the working of the Tao by simply being as totally aware of what is happening to me and around me as I am able. I try to be receptive to the gentle guidance of the supreme spirit, so that I may follow my own personal Tao (path) through life.

I am most fortunate in being able to help people by teaching them T'ai Chi and the other Taoist arts. It gives me great pleasure and makes me feel very humble to be of service to others in this way. I thank God for the gifts he gave me that allow me to do this work when I say my prayers.

So is Taoism occult? Yes and No.   Is Taoism a religion? Yes and No.

As nothing is totally Yin or totally Yang, Taoism is neither an occult practice nor a religion, yet it does contain elements of these. But Taoism is primarily 'The Way,' the natural order of things. A person once having learnt to accept the Tao of their own life finds that their existence becomes more exciting than ever before. Such people find themselves in complete awe of the beauty and diversity in the world and the universe of which we are a part. The pleasure of being allowed to witness the wonder of it all is the greatest gift anyone could ever be given. This is what the Tao (God) gives to us all. Be eternally grateful and express your gratitude in your prayers and by helping others when you can.

T'ai Chi Ch'uan

The Chinese people have been practising the art of T'ai Chi Ch'uan for centuries. In fact it is practised to such an extent that, in the past, it has drawn the bewildered attention of tourists. All over China and in Hong Kong too, many Chinese rise early to practise their T'ai Chi movements in the park, on the roof tops, in car parks and on balconies, in fact anywhere they can find a bit of space. Some people practise in groups and some prefer to practise alone. Many people in the west are under the impression that T'ai Chi is only for the elderly. This is incorrect. Ideally, T'ai Chi should be taught from an early age. For the last twenty three years I have been practising the Taoist Arts which originated in China. I have found T'ai Chi Ch'uan particularly helpful. T'ai Chi is excellent for reducing mental stress, and also for reducing tension in the muscles of the body.

The 'T'ai Chi form' is a sequence of movements which are performed in a standing position. The movements are slow and graceful, they are also a splendid therapeutic exercise. After having mastered a few movements of the T'ai Chi form, as you practise, the muscles of the body will start to relax. The mind, because it is required to focus on the physical movements, stops racing from one thought to another. The mind now starts to become calm. With a little regular practice (anything worthwhile requires a little effort), you will develop a feeling of serenity. This is why T'ai Chi is often described as 'Meditation with Movement'. Newcomers to T'ai Chi often ask, "What are the benefits of T'ai Chi?"

This is a difficult question to answer because Tai' Chi means different things to different people. There are social benefits. You will join a class where you will practise with other students. You will in time form new friendships, though some people of course will do this quicker than others. However, no matter how shy you are, if you continue to attend the class, you will develop new friends amongst the other people there, because you will all have something in common. You will improve your general health because the exercise,s whilst being gentle in application, are dynamic in their effect on the body and mind. You will improve your physical well-being. Your mind will become sharper. You will find you are able to concentrate for longer and you will develop a calmer temperament.

There are many more benefits to be gained by the practice of T'ai Chi but these are best left for the time being. You must 'first learn to walk before you learn to run'. Most people are familiar with this saying, but I wonder if you have realized that you cannot walk properly until you can stand properly, in other words keep your balance. T'ai Chi can teach you to be a more balanced person, physically, mentally and, if you choose to take the path, spiritually.

T'ai Chi Ch'uan is usually translated to mean the 'Supreme Ultimate', an apt description. Over the years I have learnt, and I am still learning, many things about myself which have helped me to understand myself and others better. The depth of understanding one can obtain from the practice of T'ai Chi Ch'uan is inexhaustible. This knowledge is not an intellectual study only, or a physical study only, or a spiritual study only, but a harmonious combination of them all. The regular practice of T'ai Chi will develop the individual into a more balanced person, enabling them to appreciate themselves, others and the world we live in to a much greater degree.

This harmony of mind, body and spirit bring great happiness and good health to the practitioner, but it has to be earned. The more effort you put into the practice, the more you will get out of it. This does not mean that you should be very intense about your practice. On the contrary this would restrict your development. You should dedicate yourself to your practice in a relaxed manner with a feeling of exhilaration.

When you start to learn the T'ai Chi form your concentration is focused on imitating the movements of the instructor. You have to learn where to place the hands and feet, where the weight is, more on one foot than the other. Are the hands held in the correct position for the posture shown? So, at first, whilst you are beginning to learn, the form has a rather robotic quality. The instructor pauses after each posture giving you time to observe the correct positions of hands and feet. After you become more familiar with the movements the instructor will ask you to perform a posture and then walk round correcting hand and foot positions, checking your stance, making sure you are not leaning this way or that way, helping you to obtain an upright posture. In this way the student learns to feel what their body feels like when it is in the correct position. This is a very important part of the initial training. The students must learn to pay attention to themselves, not look around and think this or that person is not doing it correctly?', but concentrating their minds on what they are doing. In this way, the students learn to ground themselves, to become aware of their own reality, to feel what they are doing, to start to make efforts to bring the mind under control. This is not obvious to the student at the time. They merely concentrate on perfecting the physical movements of the form. The real work they are doing on themselves is hidden from them. That is one of the unique qualities of T'ai Chi. It is possible to practice the physical movements of the form, having no interest in its mental or spiritual value. Yet through the practice one gains benefits in these areas, whether one is aware of it or not. For what one does physically affects one mentally and also spiritually. These three aspects are composite factors that make up every human being, and if you affect one area you affect the others.

Some students are only concerned with learning the form as quickly as possible, Hell-bent on number crunching, becoming agitated if they feel they are not being taught quickly enough. This is due no doubt to the competitive attitude that is fostered in us from an early age in the western world. This is a shame, because this attitude, if it persists, will severely restrict the student's development.

If you want to learn to type and you decide to learn properly from the start, you must learn to touch type. You will find the initial effort hard and with little apparent reward. Others who taught themselves to type using two fingers may laugh at your efforts, suggesting that you give up, and do it the easy way. However, if you persist diligently, eventually you will be able to type much more efficiently than you ever would using two fingers. This fact may be hotly disputed by the two finger brigade.

So it is if you persist with your T'ai Chi training. Resist the temptation to go off and learn something new as soon as you start to feel a little bored because you have to repeat the same movements you think (and I stress you think), you know. Then you will not miss the opportunity to develop internally, an opportunity to learn how to become one with yourself. If you dash off to another class you will become bored again soon, and have to move on again., learning a little of many things, but nothing of any substance. You may gain lots of external experience and knowledge, but you will gain little experience and knowledge of your inner self. You cannot relate this experience and knowledge that you have gained to others and your surroundings because you do not understand who you are. You must come to know yourself first before you can know others.

The practise of T'ai Chi will put you in touch with your physical body. You will become aware of the muscle changes that take place when you step forwards, backwards, sidewards, lift a leg into the air in a kicking action, bend at the waist, and so on. It will teach you to be aware of your own unnecessary excessive use of energy. You will learn how to move your body more naturally, more efficiently, using up less energy as you do so. This will give you a greater reserve of energy to draw on in times of stress. Your temperament will improve and you will become a happier person.

This awareness of your own reality through an understanding of your own physical body is essential. This physical body that you inhabit is the vehicle with which you drive through life. To be able to pay attention to the journey you must be able to operate the vehicle without using all your energy to do so. So the more effort you put in when you learn to drive, the less effort you will need to drive the car efficiently when you set out on your journey. You are in charge of your vehicle, and you must be responsible for its fuel, oil and water. You must watch out for any excessive wear, and you must carry out maintenance should the road of life throw up unexpected obstacles in your path which cause damage to your vehicle. After a while, when you have gained a little experience of driving your vehicle, you begin to feel the road through the steering mechanism. It's as though you can feel the contact the tyres have with the road. You have become one with your vehicle. Sitting in the centre of your vehicle, you feel what it feels, as it travels down the road. At first when you pass your test your attention is focused never too far away from the front of the car. Obstacles seem to come upon you suddenly, your heart pounds in your chest, your mind races as you struggle to control your vehicle and negotiate the obstacle, expending much energy in the process. As you become more experienced and relaxed, your gaze moves further in front of the vehicle as it travels along. You are however perfectly well aware of the conditions just in front of your vehicle.

Your greater efficiency and the relaxed manner with which you now handle your vehicle allows you to be aware of a greater proportion of the road before you. Now, you can see obstacles and adverse conditions in good time. Now, you are able to adjust your position and speed in good time without the sudden panic. You are in better control of your vehicle. You have a much greater awareness of the road before you. You use less energy during the journey and are therefore able to travel further before becoming fatigued. As you learn more of your vehicle's abilities and limitations you become more and more aware, and you suffer less and less stress as you drive around. Your body is the vehicle with which you may travel through life. If it is badly maintained, constantly supplied with the incorrect grade of fuel and oil, it will not serve you efficiently for long. Your awareness of your journey through life will be restricted and dull by comparison. So learn to look after your body. Feed it the correct fuel and oil, supply it with good quality water, pay attention to its maintenance and it will serve you well; then you will have a good journey. There will still be times of stress, but you will have ample supplies of energy to cope with these low points in your life. Then you will start to appreciate the uniqueness of your own path in life, the beauty of the world around you and your contribution to it, however humble that contribution may be. You will see obstacles and dangers approaching and negotiate them with greater care, ever developing greater awareness and confidence in your ability to control your vehicle on the journey of life.

There is a saying that most people, if walking down a path, in a country that is unfamiliar to them, encounter a fast flowing river, jump in with the intention of getting to the other side: a Taoist jumps in and swims with the flow to see where it will take him. So as I drive my vehicle down the path of life I feel the road as best I can. I try to develop my awareness so that I can perceive the road ahead, for I have never travelled this road before. I have travelled others like it, and the road sometime looks familiar, but I know it is not the same. This is just my mind trying to take control. The mind is like an unruly child, it forms thoughts and tries to convince you that this is reality, when it is in fact, fantasy. I don't know through what type of country or terrain my journey will lead me. When I come to a fork in the road or a crossroad I rely on a balance of the knowledge I have gained from past experience and intuition (feel) to guide me in the right direction. If the road then runs through rough country I no longer wonder if it would have been better to take another path. I remember the words of a wise man I once had the pleasure to speak with. He told me a simple truth that I have many times had reason to remember: 'THE PAST IS IRRETRIEVABLE.'

The place where I am now at along my journey is the only thing that matters. It is where I am now. That is my reality. Anything else conjured up by the mind is illusion and fantasy.

The T'ai Chi Form is usually split into a series of numbers. For instance, the Lee family style that I practise is divided into 50 movements for the short form and 140 movements for the complete form. This is a breakdown of the 42 sequences which make up the long form. These sequences have beautiful names such as 'Play the Guitar', and 'The Fair Lady Weaving', which were devised some 1500 years ago, and in turn were developed from the original eight postures, which came into being around 10,000 years ago. They are broken down into numbers as these are more easily assimilated by people of the west than are the sequences.

So how does the T'ai Chi Form help us to develop an ability to exist in the present? Well, when the students are practising for instance No 7, if they allow their minds to wander to No 9, which is often the case, for as I stated earlier, the mind is like an unruly child and must be disciplined, then they are not giving their attention to No 7, which is the movement that they are at present performing. The mind eager for more knowledge races ahead impatient to know more, separating itself from the present and losing touch with the body. The mind enters the world of fantasy and illusion and leaves the reality of the present. This will become obvious to the instructor quite soon as the correctness of movement No 7 rapidly starts to deteriorate. The students will be asked to practise the incorrect parts over and over again in an endeavour to correct the situation and bring the students back to themselves. At first, students usually find this quite irritating as they wish to push on, learning more and more numbers. The instructor will start to move amongst the students now, correcting a posture here and a hand or foot movement there. Soon the students start to turn their attention inwards towards themselves. The repetition of movements they think (and again I stress they think), they know eventually brings them to an awareness of their own illusions. Through being constantly corrected by the instructor, the students start to pay greater attention to their own movements as they perform them, and less attention to the movements to come, which is the future and has not yet arrived. And by this training they are made aware of their own reality. They are encouraged to become one with themselves and to be aware of their own immediate actions, aware of their own presence, now. The student by this process strengthens the mind and starts to bring it under their control.

As the training continues and the student progresses, out of this progression is born another problem. Now the students are more aware of their own actions, as they perform for instance No 12, and are aware that perhaps this time they did not perform it as well as they did previously. If they are working on their own they can stop and practise the movement again a few times to correct any faults. If however, they are practising with a group that is practising up to say No 30, this is not possible because the group must keep together, their movements synchronized as closely as possible. Because they are dedicated and are trying to learn the form correctly, they may become angry with themselves, and they think of their mistakes as they continue with the movements. Therefore as they practise 13,14,15 and so on, whilst still thinking of No 12 and analysing what went wrong, they are living in the past, angry with themselves for performing No 12 badly. They forget their own reality again and become consumed with the past, which cannot be relived; the past is irretrievable. They lose contact with the present again. So they have another problem. They may feel that they have not improved at all. But of course they have learnt much about themselves, and of course there is much more that can be learned. The depth of learning that can be gleaned from the practise of T'ai Chi is like the ocean. There are some parts that man has as yet not been able to explore. As with the physical and the metaphysical, the material and the sentient, the seen and the unseen, man's development continues. Time is not important, but how we use it is. A student may see this new problem as some kind of failure on their part. Failure is only a stepping stone to success. This problem that has arisen can be solved.

Now students have learnt a little of the T'ai Chi Form, developed their stances, hand and foot movements to a good standard. They are ready to practise making these movements flow together, following the instructor who sets the pace the students follow trying to make the form flow, trying to blend each movement into the next so that the movements all become one long movement without any pauses or breaks, and at the same time keeping together with the group, so the whole group moves as one. This is very difficult to achieve but on the occasions that this is successful, it is a beautiful thing to see. As an instructor I have had the pleasure of witnessing the scene many times, yet when it happens it never fails to warm my heart. An even greater experience is to be a part of that group and experience it at first hand. Students when they first experience this are enthralled. Working together as a group. A bunch of individuals striving together with a common goal. Sacrificing their individuality for the common good, and putting their heart and soul into it. It is an experience that can not be put into words, it can only be felt:

'IT IS ONLY WITH THE HEART THAT ONE CAN SEE RIGHTLY;

WHAT IS ESSENTIAL IS INVISIBLE TO THE EYE.'

However, as I mentioned earlier, this is no mean feat. Dedicated students usually practise at home, sometimes on a daily basis to supplement the instruction they receive in class. Others practise only in the classroom, for various reasons, finding it difficult to practise at home. Soon, those who practise at home will outshine the others who do not. This may encourage those who do not practise at home to surmount their difficulties and practise on a daily basis. If they can only manage ten minutes practice a day they will derive much benefit and see a vast improvement in their performance. If the time is available, twenty minutes would be better. The benefits that will be accrued though the regular practise of the T'ai Chi Form will be in direct relation to the effort put in. The best time to practise is as soon after sunrise as you can, or just before sunset. If this is not convenient then any suitable time will do. Do not however, practise just after having a meal as the practise of the T'ai Chi Form massages the internal organs and could leave you feeling sick. Wait an hour after a light meal and two to three hours after a large meal before practising.

So we can imagine that the students who are still persevering with their studies of T'ai Chi are quite dedicated and either practise at home on a regular basis or attend two or three classes a week. The students start to become aware of themselves, concentrating on themselves, their balance, their posture, their hand and foot movements. As before out of this dedication, which is wholly necessary to their progress, comes another problem. For, steeped in their own development, they do not wish to alter any of the elements of their T'ai Chi Form. They do not wish to conform to the flow of the group but want the group to work at their speed which they consider is the only correct one. As they derive much pleasure from their own individual practice, they do not wish to change it in any way. They love their T'ai Chi Form. They have worked hard to attain this level of individual expression and they are very proud of that attainment. They love their T'ai Chi Form so much, it has become a possession, a thing that they can keep for themselves, something other people do not have. So the ego has again raised its ugly head and must be confronted and brought under control. The real T'ai Chi belongs to no one. It is available to all those who are dedicated and sincere, But it belongs to no one; it is a gift from the Tao, given to those who ask through their dedication and service.

The experienced instructor will understand these things and take it upon himself, gently if possible, to coax students into working with the group. As an individual each of us is unique. We must learn to express our individuality freely and without fear. But we exist in this world with many others and we must learn to work in co-operation with others for the common good. We must learn to control the ego so that we can express ourselves individually in our own unique way when required, yet be able to blend in and work with others for the good of the community as a whole.

Like the ants in our garden we discussed in the chapter on the Yin and Yang. We have our individual task, gatherer of food, cleaner, soldier. All have the same equal importance to the survival of the nest. The survival of the nest is paramount to the survival of the individual - But the survival of the individual is not paramount to the survival of the nest. Ants are born and die but the nest lives on. Men come and go, great leaders arise when they are needed, do their work then slip away and are forgotten. But the world lives on.

The foregoing scenario of the student's development may not necessarily follow the pattern I have outlined, there are many other combinations of the foregoing factors along with others not mentioned; this is merely one possible scenario. But, just as the yin and yang, which are separate yet combine to form the duality of everything in nature, Yin is not bad and Yang good, they are the two opposing yet complimentary factors which are inherent in everything that exists in our universe, so when the students set themselves the goal of learning good posture, stances and say the first 20 movements of the T'ai Chi Form and when that goal is achieved, you could say that is yang. However, in the process of learning the movements well and attaining this goal, they become rather robotic, which is incorrect, that is to say, yin. Following this, when the student becomes aware of their own movements and turns their attention inwards to themselves, from an individual point of view this is good, which is yang. But from a group point of view it is bad, which is yin. So, Yin and Yang oppose yet harmonize with each other. Therefore there is nothing that is good or bad really. Making the judgement that something is good or bad merely depends upon your perspective at that time, or the point of view that you hold. As you develop that perspective or point of view, it invariably changes. Just as in nature, everything is in a constant state of flux. Nothing is stationary. Not even a thought is stationary. As soon as you have it, you start to develop it, or replace it with another thought; it never remains stationary.

So it is with the T'ai Chi Form, it is never really stationary. This is only necessary as the student learns. When they have reached a certain standard they are able to progress on their own, aware of their own mistakes and shortcomings as they arise. They make no judgement that they are good or bad, but they accept their mistakes and then leave them where they belong, in the past, moving on, adding the experience to their individual pot of knowledge, developing themselves, taking responsibility for their own actions. No living in the past. No expectations of the future. Aware of their own reality which is always, always, in the present. T'ai Chi teaches the student that you cannot learn about reality only by talking about it, only by thinking or analysing it, or only reading about it. All these can be aids, but it is the practice that is the most important ingredient. T'ai Chi teaches the student the meaning of life. The meaning of life is living it. It is here - right now - in the present, nowhere else.

Whatever we say or do can under certain conditions be construed to be good, or under other conditions bad. As well as continuing to develop the material side of life through science and engineering skills, we would do well to spend a little more time developing our sentient skills, and in the process we could perhaps learn to exist together in harmony, something we will never learn to do through material development alone.

The Supreme Ultimate: an apt description of T'ai Chi, for in it are all the lessons of life. By this statement I do not imply that I know them all personally. For, whilst being an instructor, I also remain a student. I have learnt much, but there is much, much, more to learn. When I say my prayers I thank the Lord for the gifts I have been given, including the material gifts of food, clothing and shelter that we all need. I do not have a great deal of the material possessions of life by some people's standards in this country. Yet I have great wealth compared to others in other countries around the world. I have enough for my needs and I am deeply grateful for that.

Speaking for myself I practised the T'ai Chi Form for between 30 and 45 minutes every day, minus Christmas and Boxing Day, for fifteen years. There were times during this period that my practice had an austerity to it that now, when I am reminded of it by some incident, causes me to smile to myself. Still it was, I am sure, a necessary part of my development. I no longer practise as an individual on a daily basis, as I now teach T'ai Chi on most days. But I still find time for a little individual practice on a regular basis, practising going over parts of the form that I feel need polishing up a little. I consider this very necessary because I believe that 'He who thinks he has nothing more to learn has not learnt much'. A conceited man does not know or see the truth. This kind of practice is of a purely physical nature, yet it is still of great value.

The regular practice of the T'ai Chi form has taught me many things, one of which is that to have an attitude towards my practice that is too austere, is to become a prisoner to it. The loss of form is freedom. However, understanding this mentally is not enough, one must live it to know it. True knowledge only comes through direct experience. Therefore, a dedicated attitude to the precision and correctness of your practice is essential, for it is a necessary place to pass through on your journey to freedom. A man who has not experienced restriction cannot appreciate true freedom. True freedom comes from within.

When the activities of others are not seen as aggressive acts that stop us from doing what we wish to do. When we can accept what life gives us without labelling it good or bad, learning to work within this framework without letting the emotions rise up, causing us to lose control. Then we can have true freedom. Then we can follow the way (Tao). Then we can do what we wish because we know who we really are and what we should do. When we no longer succumb to greed, ambition and desire. When we have rid ourselves of these things which dull our senses and blind us to reality. Then we shall know true freedom. Greed, ambition and desires, these things are the restrictions, and they come from within each of us, not from external sources. So we must work on our interior, purify our bodies and minds. Then we will have true freedom and enjoy a peace and harmony only dreamed of by others. It can be done, but only you can do it, no one else can do it for you. Life on this earth can be Heaven or Hell. The choice is yours.

Many years ago, the idea of teaching T'ai Chi professionally to others seemed repugnant to me. Passing on the beauty of T'ai Chi and the other Taoist arts for money seemed sacrilegious (as I mentioned I was rather austere about my T'ai Chi at one time). Yet I had received so much from the practice of these arts that I felt duty bound to try to make this available to others. It was at this point that I realized that I had the same problem that I described earlier. I was like the student who holds on to movement No 12 when he is actually performing No 13 or14. I was bogged down by my knowledge of the past. In those days, when a person wished to learn, he would find a master and try to persuade him to teach them. If successful, they, in return for their training, would perform some service for the master, often of a domestic nature. The student would devote all his time to his practices and service. This of course is not possible nowadays as life has changed much since those days. People go to work and are paid for their labours and then they choose what to spend their money and leisure time on. As a T'ai Chi instructor I have to live too, so I charge for the services I provide, and I try to give good value in return. I make no judgement on the right or wrong of it. I just accept that that is how it is. If I am to help people by teaching the Taoist Arts, which I believe is my humble contribution to humanity, I must charge for this service. This is the reality of the modern world in the west, which is where I am. So I give to those that are interested in the Taoist arts, and they in turn give to me coins that I may provide for my basic needs. We both give to each other and we both receive from each other. By this process I am useful to society.

I am indeed fortunate to be able to make my living doing something which at the same time gives me great personal satisfaction, the opportunity to make a contribution to the health and well-being of other people, and at the same time also allows me to be of service to God. Perhaps I was born lucky because the Lord rains gifts on me constantly. The longer I practise the Taoist arts the luckier I seem to become. My own life becomes more and more beautiful and exciting, as I learn not to resist the flow but to follow my own personal Tao(way).

Self Defence

Much has been written about T'ai Chi and self defence. Within the Taoist Arts Association that I belong to T'ai Chi and self defence are taught separately. Some people prefer to study T'ai Chi only considering the self defence aspect as a form of aggression, whilst others will practise self defence, but consider T'ai Chi too soft to be of any practical use as a form of self defence. Others study both together.

My views on T'ai Chi are given in the previous chapter. In this chapter I would like to discuss the self defence aspect in isolation. I will start by explaining how I came to study these arts. In 1974, six years after leaving the Army, I was working as an insurance agent and felt the need to have a hobby which provided some exercise. Since most of my working day was either spent in an office, sitting in someone's home, or sitting behind the wheel of my car driving to the next call, it was not surprising I was slightly overweight and not very fit. I decided to improve my physical condition. The question was how. I did not like running. Just pounding around mile after mile did not appeal to me at all, and being born under the astrological sign of Gemini I needed mental stimulation as well. Sports like football, cricket and rugby did not really fit the bill, and these were seasonal. I needed something I could practise all year round, something to get my teeth into, something physically and intellectually stimulating. There were a lot of kung fu films about at the time and I noticed an advert in the local paper advertising a Kung Fu class for beginners, which invited people interested in joining to attend for an interview at a local hotel. I decided to go along and see what it was all about. I had not at that time seen any of the Kung Fu films myself as I was working until 8 o' clock most nights, but my friends had told me about them. I had learnt some self defence during combat training while I was in the Army, and the stories I was told did not seem to be realistic. I was aware that the films would have to be larger then life to be entertaining to the public. Keeping fit whilst learning Kung Fu, which would be useful as a means of self defence, seemed much more appealing than jogging. At the appointed time I arrived at the hotel. A notice in the lobby directed applicants upstairs to the second floor. As I was a little early I took the stairs rather than the lift. If I was going to get fit, I may as well start now. I arrived on the second floor to find an enormous queue right down the corridor. There were fifteen or so seats which were occupied and a few people standing. I tagged on to the end of the queue and waited. Presently a man came out of the interview room followed by about twelve people. The man apologized for the delay then asked the first twelve people to enter the interview room. Smiling, he bade the rest of us take the seats vacated by these people and asked us to wait, explaining we would only have to wait ten minutes. He turned and went into the interview room.

Twenty minutes later the door opened and out filed the previous batch followed by the interviewer smiling. "Sorry to keep you waiting. Please come in," he said. Eleven others and myself filed in. We sat round a large oval table. The man introduced himself and we were told a little of the history of the style. We were then informed membership must be obtained before we could begin training. This would cost £10, payable now. The fee for a lesson would be £1 payable on the night. The interviewer, who was also an instructor, after having collected as many £10s as he could, allocated people to Thursday or Friday evening, depending on their choice, adding that they would receive their membership cards on their first training night. From those who did not have ten pounds with them he took a small deposit, saying the balance must be paid along with the lesson fee on the first night's training.

Not having the ten pounds required myself, I paid a deposit of five pounds to secure a place on a Friday evening for the 9 o' clock to 10 o' clock session. This suited me as I didn't finish my calls until around 8-30pm on a Friday, leaving me just enough time to get to the training hall. Those who either did not have any money or who did not wish to join then, wanting to think about it first, were told Thursday evening was now full, but they were welcome to come along on Friday evening, and if the class was not full they could join then, strictly on a first come first served basis. There were to be four sessions each night between 6 o' clock and 10 o' clock. The instructor informed us that the following week would be the first training session.

Standing up he said. "Thank you gentlemen, I will see you next week at the training hall." Walking to the door, he opened it and smiling said, "Goodbye," and out we all filed.

I was impressed by his efficiency. If the training was as good I would be well pleased.

The following Friday night I arrived ten minutes early to find a few people waiting in the corridor outside the Training Hall. I was told by one of these that the instructor had told them not to enter until 9 o' clock exactly. We took it in turns to peep through the small window to watch the training session, the students were being taught a set form of movements which they performed over and over. At 8-55pm precisely, the class was stopped and the students were told to get changed. Then at 9 o' clock precisely, we were invited into the Hall and told to change quickly.

We were organized into lines, and then the instructor demonstrated an exercise once or twice.Then we were told to repeat it until told to stop. The instructor walked round as we repeated the exercises, shouting at various individuals in an effort to make them work harder. The exercise session lasted for twenty five minutes and included such things as press-ups on the fingers and the back of the wrists, sit ups, the splits. Anybody who complained or was not working hard enough (according to the instructor's definition of hard work) was told if they did not want to train they should get changed and go. This aggressive authoritarian attitude did not really bother me too much as I had been treated in a similar manner by the physical training instructors during my time in the Army. However one or two people did not like it and left. The warm up and exercise session completed the instructor demonstrated a block in defence to a punch to his head. We then spent the next fifteen minutes practising this with a partner, taking it in turns to strike with a punch or block the punch. Most people found it difficult to keep repeating the same exercise over and over again, but the instructor walked around repeating his previous statement 'if you don't want to train get changed and leave' to anyone who stopped for more than a few seconds. For the last five minutes we were instructed in the set form of hand movements we had seen the previous group practising. Then the instructor told us to line up again and we bowed in a manner shown to us by him and he told us that the training would get harder. If we expected to be like Bruce Lee (the star of the Kung Fu movies) after a few sessions we would be disappointed, as such skill would take many years of very hard training, and if we wished to learn Kung Fu we would have to train very hard and train regularly. There was no easy way.

On the way out I chatted to my training partner, who suggested calling in the pub for a quick drink, so off we went to the nearest pub. I both drank and smoked in those days. We had a good chat in the pub and had more than one drink as well, telling ourselves we were replacing lost body fluids. Going for a drink after the training session turned into a regular thing. As the weeks went by he started to complain to me that the training session consisted of twenty five minutes of exercises and only thirty minutes training in the techniques, five minutes being reserved for us to get changed. After ten weeks, this amounted to only four hand and arm blocks as a counter to a punch, and two hand blocks as a counter to a front kick, plus the set form we were learning. I did not find this a problem myself, as I felt I still had plenty of room for improving my techniques, but I had to admit that I felt half an hour a week training was not long enough.

Two weeks later, he came to the training session excitedly telling me of another Kung Fu club he had heard about and asked me if I would go to have a look at it with him the following Monday night. I was not really all that bothered, but he persisted and I eventually agreed to go with him the following Monday.

We arrived at the club, which was conducted in the concert hall of a social club at 8-30pm. The session was well under way, as they had started training at 7-30pm. We spoke to the instructor, who said we were welcome to join the following week if we wished. The training session was for two hours and cost only 50p. We asked if we might be allowed to watch the training, and he told us we could watch as long as we wished. The instructor mentioned that the bar opened for them at 9-30pm. If we wished to wait we could have a chat to some of the students who stopped for a drink before going home. This sounded good to us. Having the opportunity to talk to some of the students in a friendly environment seemed a great idea, and the excuse to have a pint as well. What more could one ask for? We settled down to watch. The students were training in a strange way. They were practising a kind of attack and defence movement. One person struck, the other defended the blow, then immediately struck back and the partner defended this blow then struck again. This was done in a continuous flowing way that looked graceful and natural. The students only stopped when they lost the rhythm. They first composed themselves then continued. This system of training we were told later was known as rollaways, and it was performed slowly and continuously. But what made it so intriguing to me was the fact that they did it with their eyes closed. Later they practised arm and wrist locks and also set forms. They also practised kicks, and these were always practised with a partner in a system I was later to discover was called foot flow patterns. The atmosphere was pleasant and the students looked as if they were enjoying the training. The instructors (there were three others apart from the chief instructor we spoke to) were firm but not authoritarian in their instruction. I decided to train at this club on a Monday evening and also at the other one on a Friday evening. My training partner, who I now regarded as a friend preferred to train at the new club only. He tried to sway me to do the same but I was adamant. I wished to try both systems. However, I soon found that it was not possible to mix the training. One being a soft internal style, which relied on speed, suppleness, physical and mental dexterity and the internal energy Chi as the power source, and the other being a hard external style which relied on physical strength requiring development of the physique. The application of the techniques was vastly different. I decided to concentrate my efforts on the soft internal style, which suited my physique and temperament better. I was also able to train for two nights a week instead of one because they had another club on a Tuesday in the same hall. Three months later I attended a weekend course to take my first grading. This course had to be held at a larger hall because people came from other areas and The Grand Master, Professor Chee Soo, would take the course. I was very excited about seeing a real Kung Fu Master. I remember waiting to see him enter the training hall. I had a picture in my mind of a strong powerful man. When he entered the hall I was greatly surprised, almost shocked, for in came a very small Chinese man with a big smile across his face. Apart from the fact he was Chinese he looked just like any other pleasant middle aged man, not at all like I imagined a Kung Fu Master would look like. He certainly did not look tough, as I had expected. But later that day I was to learn that this small pleasant Chinese man, was as tough as they come. As I watched him demonstrate various techniques during the day with the senior instructors, many of whom had been training in other martial arts for many years, I was enthralled as I watched him evade their blows with graceful, balletic movements. But what stirred my imagination most was his composure. Whilst his opponents at times showed great agitation and aggression, he remained completely non-aggressive. He seemed somehow empty, and yet at the same time he had great depth. I knew then that there was something I had to learn from this man, but I had no idea what it was.

For me, learning Kung Fu has been like peeling an onion. Once you have removed the outer skin, to see what it holds within, you find the onion stings the eyes slightly and makes them water. If you want to understand its depth you must peel off another layer, knowing when you do the onion will sting the eyes more. Intentional suffering in the pursuit of knowledge. As with the onion, each time as I have peeled away a layer to look deeper within myself, what I have learnt has brought tears to my eyes. But I must be brave and continue to peel away the layers and erase my illusions, fears and negative emotions. I must peel away the layers one by one until there is nothing left, until I have annihilated myself (the ego) then I too will be a master, but I know this will take many, many years, perhaps more than this lifetime.

Over the years I have had to travel about the country to train under him as he has moved from one location to the next. I still travel to Bristol and South Wales, were he now lives, on a regular basis to train under him. Although he is now in his seventy fifth year he can still out manoeuver me because he has trained for over sixty years to my twenty and I cannot match his awareness and mental control, which more than make up for the decline in his physical abilities. Fifteen years ago, in a rare private moment I shared with him, he told me the main reason for his fascination with the Taoist Arts over the years was that you were finding out about yourself, no one else, just yourself. As with many things he has told, or has shown me, it was many years before I understood the true meaning of what he was saying to me.

A master craftsman can take a piece of rough metal and heat it in a fire, beat it with a hammer and fashion it into a fine sword. This fine sword in the hands of a master swordsman can be used not to show off his skill, or exercise his will over others by force (that is egotism), but to protect the weak from harm should it be necessary.

Many years ago I stopped trying to fight my opponent and engaged in a battle of epic proportions against the most devious, vicious and cunning opponent on earth, myself.

I have always considered Kung Fu an Art of Self Defence not a Martial Art. To me there is a great difference between the two. Martial means warfare - warlike - fond of fighting. Self defence is described in my dictionary as an aggressive act, intended as defence. If we take the word aggressive not to mean forceful or hostility, but self-assertive, which is one of it meanings, then you will be able to understand the definition I place on self defence. To clarify, if someone uses physical force against you, you should, if you practise an art of self defence, give in to their physical force, which will negate it. In the process of applying force against you, your opponent will have sacrificed his own balance, creating a weakness within himself, which you, by giving in to his force, are in a position to take advantage of. The above applies to verbal and mental aggression as well as physical aggression. Aggression is like the onion, there are layers upon layers, and whilst it is easy (oh so easy) to see this in others, not many are prepared to look for the aggression in themselves, but it is there nevertheless, and needs to be tackled as it severely colours our judgement of reality, and of others' actions.

Self defence, to me, is not about fighting. I do not wish to fight anybody. But I do wish to learn how to defend myself against force, be it physical, verbal or mental. Force has always been used to oppress people around the world, and we are all guilty. It is no good blaming the Russians, Chinese, Germans or Japanese or anyone else for the atrocities committed in the past. We committed terrible deeds in the crusades and many times since. So all nationalities are guilty of cruel crimes against their fellow man. But there is light at the end of the tunnel, for who would have thought that the Berlin Wall would come down and Russia would co-operate so willingly for world peace?

Over the years during my training in Kung Fu I have met many people who seemed, at first, to be extremely aggressive. Many of them, once I had come to know them a little better, often turned out to be extremely nice people, who merely acted or spoke aggressively to cover their sensitive nature, afraid to show their true self for fear of being taken advantage of. When these people train in the internal arts of Kung Fu they eventually lose this aggression and become very interesting people from whom much can be learned, for we are each unique in our background and experience of life, and sensitive people learn more readily than others. This does not mean that these people become timid, on the contrary, their aggression is replaced by self assertiveness. They have the self confidence to stand up for themselves. If attacked physically or verbally, they are now able to elude their aggressiveness which is often seen as an affront by others. Instead, they now appear as pleasant cheerful individuals to others and thereby reduce the possibility of conflict. So, not only have they changed, the world and the people in it appear to have changed also.

However, before you can do this, you must first recognize that you are aggressive. If you think that you are not an aggressive person, then the chances are that you are. We can all be aggressive under certain conditions, and before you can learn to control your aggression, you must first learn to recognize when that aggression rises in you. It is no good saying it is the other persons fault. They should not have spoken to you in that way, or done what ever it is that has annoyed you. If, for example, you were supposed to prepare the evening meal for yourself and your partner because your partner would be arriving home later than you, and, lets assume, for some unavoidable reason you were home later then expected. When your partner arrives home, and the meal is not ready, they may well be upset and complain vehemently. If you retaliate saying perhaps. in a raised voice, it is not your fault and they should not talk to you that way what tends to happen is that the situation escalates into a slanging-match, which only serves to aggravate the situation. Both partners are reacting aggressively now. Perhaps both have had irritating problems to deal with during the day that have left them exhausted, and now tired and hungry they attack each other, each one laying the blame on the other. Eventually one will give in, but the other will be full of resentment, firstly for having lost the conflict and secondly because they believe the other was to blame anyway. If on the other hand, one or both of them has learnt to deal with their own aggression the situation could have gone differently. The first partner home would be in the process of preparing the meal when the second partner arrived. On finding the evening meal was not yet ready they would most probably enquire why, this enquiry would be in a more moderate tone than in the previous example. The first partner would state the reason for their unavoidable delay in arriving home on time and that would be the end of the matter. Even if the enquiry as to why the meal was not ready was delivered vehemently, if the other partner states the reason for the delay in a moderate tone, explaining that it was beyond their control, recognizing their partner's aggression as the result of a tiring day at work and suggesting they rest while the meal is prepared, they absorb the aggression and restore balance.

An art of self defence uses the same principles. Students are taught to give in to force at all times. If a blow is aimed at your head by your opponent's fist, students are taught not to raise an arm and block the blow, but to make contact with a hand or arm, then giving in to the force of the blow, redirect it. This creates an imbalance in your opponent that you can take advantage of. In terms of the principles of yin and yang. The delivered blow is yang. When the blow has reached its full extent, then for a split second, just before the opponent retracts his arm the strike turns to yin. His balance has been sacrificed, his force is spent, and he is now weak. You on the other hand, when you gave in to the force of the blow, which was yin on your part, are still in control of your balance. Therefore when he becomes weak (yin), you become strong (yang), and at this point have the opportunity to counter attack in the second that it will take him to recover his balance.

If you plunge your hand into water it gives way to the intrusion, and when you retract your hand it fills the space immediately. When in motion, if it meets an obstruction it flows round it, if this is not possible it remains within the restriction and builds up its reserves until it can flow over it or change direction taking another path, adapting to changing circumstances with complete acceptance. Water is the most yielding substance on earth, yet nothing can withstand its force. Given time water will even wear away rock.

In the soft style of kung Fu that we practise, the training is designed to eradicate aggression because aggression serves to place a cocoon around a person. The cocoon severely restricts your movements and it blinds you to the reality of our world. If you can break out of this cocoon you become like the butterfly, able to move freely about your business and able to perceive the world on a vast scale compared to the caterpillar, freeing yourself from fear and opening yourself to the wonder of the world. If someone is aggressive towards you, be tolerant, they deserve your sympathy, for they will only hurt themselves in the long run. Do not retaliate. Give in to their force.

BE GENTLE AND YOU WILL NEED NO STRENGTH

In the soft arts, we train ourselves to be sensitive to our opponents' intentions. However, before we can learn to be sensitive to our opponents' intentions, we must first become sensitive to ourselves. This training starts with what to the novice seems easy at first. STANCES. The importance of stance is often overlooked by the student. Basically, a stance is given a particular name and denotes whether the body weight is evenly distributed between both legs, or whether more weight is on one leg or the other, and if one leg is bent whilst the other is straight, and so on. The names given to these stances are often of animals which mimic these positions naturally. Examples are, the crane stance, where one leg is raised in the air, bent at the knee, whilst the weight is being supported by the other leg; the frog stance, which requires the student to sit on his haunches, feet flat on the ground, like a frog. To start with, the student is shown a stance by the instructor and the student copies the position. In the beginning, the student usually thinks stances are just something that have to be learnt to pass the grading syllabus. If he is given a technique to practise, all thought of correct stance and posture are forgotten.

Learning kung Fu can be likened to learning how to read and write. Firstly, before we can read or write the words, we must learn the letters of the alphabet. This is the boring bit that is hard to concentrate on. We must learn the letters of the alphabet, parrot fashion. Only then can we learn to understand how these letters go together to make words. This is not easy for the beginner, as one is given various rules and told that these rules must be obeyed to obtain the correct result, but sometimes the rules do not apply one is told. All very confusing in the beginning. These rules must be understood and the exceptions learnt, as otherwise one's writing would be incomprehensible to others. Without correct stances none of the techniques practised by the student will work in reality. Like the letters' the stances must fit together to form a continuous movement, which is the technique.

Just as the letters, each in its correct order, go together to make up the words, when you can write words you can learn how to construct sentences, then paragraphs. After that, if you wish to further develop your writing, you may wish to learn to write business letters, articles, reports. There is no end to the skills you can develop with your writing. Of course, not everyone will want to develop their skills to this degree, and of course how far they develop these skills is up to them. So it is with Kung Fu. There is no end to the skills that can be developed. Some people practise for a year or so then drift away. Others carry on, each making his or her own choice. It is not that one choice is right and the other wrong, they are just different choices. We must each follow our own path, trying not to judge others along the way, instead, learning to understand ourselves and the part we play within our society.

So we are back to ourselves again. Back to basics. And, like the stance we are trying to learn, once we have learnt the basic stance then we find that there is more to it than we thought. We have learnt to appreciate where our weight is, either more on one leg than the other, or evenly spread between them both. Now we can consider were the weight is, on the foot or feet as the case may be. Is it mostly on the little toe edge, the instep, the ball of the foot or the heel? When this is done we can look at our posture. Is the back straight without tension in the muscles? Are we leaning slightly to the left, right, forwards or backwards? We have gone as far as we can on our own? We now need the co-operation of a partner. And this is where the fun and confusion starts. We need a partner to look at us and tell us if we are leaning this way or that way, if our feet are pointing in the right direction, because we just cannot see ourselves as others do. If we truly want to learn self defence we need the co-operation of a partner who can tell us what we look like from the outside, the position from which we can never see ourselves as others see us. This is where our problems with dealing with our own aggression start.

Let us assume we are working with a partner on our stances, taking it in turns to take up a position, whilst the other checks our posture to see if it is correct for the stance we are performing. Let us further assume that our partner is of a type who enjoys giving instructions and is perhaps a little bossy. Of course no one has a perfect posture, we are all slightly deformed. If you look closely at yourself you will see that one arm is longer then the other, one hand and one foot larger then the other. Our bossy partner is having a great time correcting our posture and issuing forth instructions, telling us to straighten up and not lean back, forwards, left or right. All this after a while may seem to be overdone and become very irritating to us. This is where it can start to turn into a battle if care is not taken. It is very tempting to complain to your partner that they are being over critical, or if you are too timid to complain, to think they are being over critical, the effect is the same, communication breaks down. We may decide we will give them a taste of their own medicine when it is our turn to evaluate their stance. We feel threatened and respond by becoming mentally or verbally aggressive. At this point, all value from the exercise it lost and we enter into conflict with our partner.

Here we have an opportunity to learn how to deal with aggression on a mental and verbal level. If, when our partner is enthusiastically pointing out our shortcomings, instead of becoming irritated by their behaviour, we genuinely try to correct our faulty posture, discussing the various points with them in a pleasant manner whilst looking for the good points that they have made, with an open mind, and a genuine wish to learn, eventually the dominant and bossy person starts to be more genuine in their criticism. However, be prepared, this may take some time. Now both people get some benefit from the exercise. Of course, you will not necessarily have a partner who is determined to be dominant or bossy. You may get a partner who is too timid to tell you what you are doing wrong. What should you do in this situation? Well, you could think that you have a perfect posture and stance, and when it is your turn correct your partner's posture to the best of your ability. However this is a little one sided and does nothing to improve YOUR posture and stance. No, what you have to do is befriend your timid partner and encourage them to criticize you. In this sense, criticism is not used in its derogatory form but is taken to mean an analytical evaluation of something. This must be explained to the timid student so that he or she sees the criticism of a partner, where necessary, not as hostile but as helpful behaviour.

So, by the practice of a simple exercise such as the one outlined above, students learn if they are by nature dominant to control their natural tendency to be aggressive and bossy. And timid students learn to become more self assertive. Students by this process have started to become aware of their partner's intentions. After many training sessions with many different training partners students learn to recognize aggression in its subtlest forms and they learn how to deal with it before it manifests into physical action. These skills of course take some time to acquire. Only those who are dedicated, training hard, over many years reach this level. The ultimate aim is never to have to fight at all. The student's aim is to become so devoid of ego and the desire to impose his will on others that when confronted with an aggressive situation, these students are able to give in to the aggression and thereby defuse the situation. In fact, if physical confrontation takes place, which they are by now well able to deal with, they would consider that they had failed. The student learns to recognize an aggressive situation arising and steers himself and loved ones away. This does not mean he is a coward, merely that he prefers not to risk unnecessary injuries to either himself or others. Through his training he has come to love and respect all life. Cornered, with no means of escape, and called upon to protect himself, this respect for himself and all forms of life along with his belief that he has been given life by the Tao (God), and that this is a precious and most beautiful gift, are likely to make him more than a match for the aggressor.

The object of the self defence training is to develop total awareness, to be able to see all the possible outcomes of any given situation. As science is seeing through experiments, in Quantum Mechanics where the outcome to an experiment cannot with certainty be predicted, self defence trains the body and mind, bringing the mind under control so the subconscious mind can be reached which allows the intuition to shine through. The self is forgotten and therefore the response to an attack will be spontaneous. The subconscious mind can respond immediately without any analysis producing spontaneous action. The conscious mind always analyses information and therefore its concluding action is always too late and never harmonized to the attack. So one of the most important aspects of any self - defence system is to learn to control the mind and quell the ego.

Children's Self Defence

Parents of children wishing to attend a self defence class would be well advised to visit the various classes in their area before they allow their children to attend. Teachers of Judo, karate, Kung Fu and other disciplines vary enormously in their training methods and the emphasis they place on good attitude and self discipline. Parents should check that the objectives of the class match their expectations.

The heroes in many Kung Fu films are often motivated by revenge in some form, revenge for a brother, sister, father or mother. This is a shame as it gives Kung Fu and other forms of self defence a bad image. This is not surprising, teaching as it does children (and adults) who watch them, that using force against others in retaliation, and disregarding law and order is somehow honourable.

If your child returns home from school or play greatly distressed after having been bullied, for you as a parent this is a heart rending experience. It is very tempting to want to give the bully a taste of his own medicine. If you give in to this urge, you become the bully and confirm to your child that bullying others is acceptable under certain conditions.

All children must learn their place in the pecking order of their circle of friends, and any social group they enter, which includes their classmates at school. This should not be confused with bullying which is the use of strength or power to coerce others by fear, to persecute others by force or threats, or to pressure or coerce a person to do something.

Self defence is, I believe, a wonderful tool for building character, self assurance and self discipline in children. However, I do not believe that parents should force their children to attend classes. Initially, encouraging the shy timid child to go may be necessary. But if, after a few weeks they still have no interest, then perhaps some other sport or pursuit which will bring them into contact with other children of the same age should be considered as an alternative.

Unfortunately, many parents fall into the trap of encouraging their child to learn judo, karate or some form of self defence so that their child can hit back if bullied. Surely, it cannot be right to condemn a child (the bully) for attacking others, while training your own child to hit back even harder. Taught correctly, self defence can both teach children how to deal with others who are stronger than themselves, and also how to deal with those who are weaker than themselves. Strong psychological defences can be developed which will help children to withstand attempts at intimidation. All children must learn to deal with adult forms of bullying and sarcasm. Children, like adults, must learn their own limitations. Continuing to argue back, or to fight a superior, is like banging your head against a brick wall (it is painful and unproductive). You must learn to give in to the stronger force. Watch wild animals in their natural habitat. When they come into conflict with each other over territory or food, you will find that they often growl, snarl and paw at each other. If one is obviously much stronger, then the other knows instinctively that its survival depends, amongst other things, on knowing its own limitations and therefore backs off rather than risk serious injury.

If you do not choose a class with a sensible instructor, sending your child to judo, karate or some form of self defence lessons to learn to protect themselves against bullies may turn your child into a bully. Long term studies of American children have shown that children who bullied in the first grade were likely to grow into aggressive antisocial adults. Marriage problems often followed and they were more likely to use violence against their own children. Their personal relationships were poor and these people had fewer friends. They also stood a greater chance of getting into trouble with the law.

The right atmosphere is essential in a class for children. Children should be encouraged to make friends with each other. Any bullying should be dealt with quickly by the instructor. Children who have many friends are less likely to become the victims of bullying. It is the shy, lonely child who is usually picked on. There are many reasons why children are shy and timid. Some of the more obvious ones are being an only child, being small for their age or having excessively strict parents. By encouraging children to train together in a friendly atmosphere, the timid shy child can be taught how to mix with others. Learning self defence will increase their self confidence. We complain about the violence in society; much of it is blamed on our teenagers. Children learn from an early age by copying from those around them. If they see us dealing with problems by becoming aggressive and violent it is not surprising that they grow up to do the same. Many parents, especially if they are both working all day, have little time to spend with their children and often feel too tired when they get home to give them any attention. Often, to get a bit of peace, children are given money to amuse themselves or bought computers to play with. Usually, so their parents will not be bothered by the noise, the computers are set up either in another room or in the children's bedrooms. Unfortunately this means communication and social skills are not passed from parents to children. Do you know that Britain has more personal computers per head of population than any other country? Yes, even more than in America. Great eh! And what do our children do for the most part with this amazing modern invention? Zap Aliens. What a waste. Of course we should not blame the children, they are just doing what children have always done, learning about their environment by watching and copying what they see. And what they see is films showing violence against man and nature. Advertisements on television for computer software depict competition and violence, winning by any means possible, using any weapon available to destroy the enemy. The man who has the most sophisticated technological weaponry is often the hero who blasts the enemy into submission. Get the other guy before he gets you, is the motto of today's hero.

Are we breeding paranoia into our children? If there are any beings from another world out there watching us I doubt they would be in any hurry to make contact, preferring to stay at a safe distance, lest we try to Zap them.

Learning self defence is, by its very nature, a tactile art and therefore places the student in a position where he or she is confronted with reality, the real world, with live people. The student is not controlling some machine which depicts on its screen an illusion of a battle in which one is the controller of one side from a position of complete safety, only a spectator and not a real participant, where one can Zap the enemy at will without fear of getting hurt. Self defence is real. You practise it with real people, in the real world.

We live in an age where everything moves faster than before. This world with its ever expanding technology is more familiar to our children than it is to us. Many of us living in large cities as we do, among the hustle and bustle of modern life, forget that many of our children do not really appreciate, from first hand experience that is, what the real world is like. We take them for trips to fun parks with their giant roller coasters and hair raising rides. Children get just as much excitement and fun from swinging on a rope from a tree branch, or playing hide and seek games among the brushes and trees. Parents like to brag that they took their children to such and such a fun or theme park. Once having paid your entrance fee and entered the park it is considered that any accidents that occur are the responsibility of the park owners, who, being wary of bad publicity, which would be detrimental to their business, do all in their power to avoid such occurrences. Once the people have got on to a ride and it sets off, it is out of their control. They just have to sit there and enjoy it, or sit there mortified waiting for it to end. They have very little responsibility for what happens during the ride. Imagine you take your children and some of their friends out into the country for a walk in a wood. Along the walk you come across a rope attached to a tree and your children want to swing on it. As a responsible parent you would of course check the rope before you allowed them to use it, checking that it was not badly worn where it is fastened to the branch, perhaps testing it with your own weight. Then, when you are satisfied that it is reasonably safe perhaps you would allow them to use it, or perhaps you would tell them it is too dangerous. Let us assume you decide to let them swing on it.

Usually, if there is more than one child, the more adventurous one will go first whilst the others wait their turn. Some may be too frightened to have a go. After watching the others having fun however, they may decide to pluck up courage and try it for themselves. Any child who has not swung from a tree by a rope before will be nervous and anxious the first time. This is only natural. They are afraid of the dangers of the unknown. They fear they will lose control, they fear falling and hurting themselves. All perfectly rational healthy fears. Once they have taken hold of the rope and swung into the air, they and only they are in control of what happens to them. They must take responsibility for their own action. If they let go of the rope and fall there is no one else to blame but themselves. If they choose a bad line of projection, and as they swing back they collide with the tree trunk and hurt themselves, they learn to deal with this by being aware of the fact, and next time if they make the same mistake again, they learn to put their feet out first to reduce the risk of hurting themselves again. The most important thing is they have learnt to step into the unknown. They faced their fear and survived. Perhaps with a scratch or two, or sore hands from the rope, but with an increase in their self esteem. They did it on their own. Future challenges which produce anxiety and fear will be judged a little more rationally than previously, consideration of possible outcomes will be considered, the good ones as well as the bad ones, and then action will be taken.

As parents, we will not always be on hand to protect our children. They must learn to take responsibility for their own actions. They must be encouraged to develop as individuals. To learn to have the courage to make their own path in life in the knowledge that along the way there will be suffering as they learn and develop. But there will also be much accomplishment and many rewards. The future is in our children, we must be careful not to stifle their enthusiasm for life, with our own fear and paranoia of the future.

Most of us live in big towns and cities, and many do not have the opportunity to visit the countryside, which is a shame. Away from the hustle and bustle of city life, listening to the songs of the birds, watching the trees swaying in the breeze, one becomes aware that the material problems of life are just temporary, just part of the ups and downs of life: 'Whilst man comes and goes; earth abides.'

We take our children to zoos to see real animals, caged and forced to live an unnatural life, for our pleasure. Through the wonderful work of people such as Sir David Attenborough, we can see wild life programmes on television. These animals are in their natural habitat and through Sir David Attenborough unique and enthusiastic narrations we, and our children, can learn much of our planet and its inhabitants. The point I am trying to convey here is that the real world we share with many other species, and the material world we humans have created for our comfort and pleasure are indivisible. They exist side by side, each with its good and bad points. Without the invention of the television, we could not watch the wild life programmes, and of course not many of us could afford to take holidays in far off exotic places to see for ourselves the wonders of nature around the world. And without the invention of ships and the aeroplane such travel would be impossible.

Alongside the technology, which we perhaps do not appreciate as well as our growing children do, we have a duty to educate our children to respect all things in nature and other human beings; whatever their colour or creed. By learning a system of self defence which is basically non aggressive a child can learn how to deal with aggression directed at them without resorting to physical violence. They can also learn to come to terms with their own fears. The training helps to eliminate any aggression that may have built up in them during the day. Life nowadays is more stressful for our children, just as indeed it is for adults.

I would like to share with you some observations I made watching my own 11 year old daughter at play with other children at a friends house. These events took place on the same weekend. One Saturday evening I watched my daughter in the company of three other children. They had previously been playing together outside, rather noisily but congenially. Then they came indoors to play games on a computer. Within a short space of time they were all rather tense, watching the screen as each took their turn at the game. As I watched, I noticed those not involved in the game occasionally make a sudden movement of an arm or twitch which was accompanied by a sigh such as 'oh! no!' or shrieks of 'jump, duck' and 'get it quick'. Before very long they were all in a highly excited state. First verbal and then physical jostling took place, as arguments broke out as to whose turn it was. As they could not resolve the situation amicably they had to be told to put the computer away. After this was done they sat around and sulked. They started to blame one another saying it was this or that person's fault the game had to be put away. This led to more physical jostling, which led to at first a good natured rough and tumble. They all joined in and at first had a great time. However as they became more and more excited, whilst releasing the adrenalin built up in them from playing the computer games, they became a little too boisterous with each other. The good natured rough and tumble turned to violence and they had to be told to stop fighting. Shortly after this it was time for us all to depart to our various homes. On the way home my daughter and I discussed what we would do the following day. We had arranged to pick up another friend of hers after lunch. I suggested going to the seaside if it was a nice day. Her black mood was soon replaced by enthusiasm for the following day's events. The next day after lunch we picked up her friend. The weather was a little overcast and it was rather windy, but neither of these facts dampened the children's zealousness for a trip to the seaside, so off we went. When we arrived it was drizzling with rain. The children decided to go to an indoor adventure play area, which was among the amusements on the sea front. The adventure play area was not too crowded, they paid their money and in they went. It had a wonderful selection of climbing apparatus, slides and rope swings. They played non stop while I watched sedately through the window of the adjoining cafe. As I watched, I was intrigued to see my daughter passing a rope up to some smaller children so they could have a swing, these children being too small to reach the rope on their own, and I thought what a contrast to the events of the previous evening. My daughter and her friend played happily for two and a half hours in the adventure play area. Then out they came, desperate for a drink and full of excited talk about the various slides and other activities. The weather had brightened up a little now and as they drank their drink they asked if they might be allowed to play on the beach. I readily agreed as I prefer the quiet of the beach to the noise of the amusements. As I waited for them to finish their drinks I wondered if they would have been as relaxed, happy and contented if they had spent the last two and a half hours in the amusement arcade playing with the machines. I came to the conclusion they would not. I also came to the conclusion that I wouldn't either, and I would no doubt have been a lot poorer too after spending two and a half hours in the amusement arcade with them. Their drinks finished, off we went to the beach. Once on the beach they took their shoes and socks off and ran shrieking in and out of the water. We walked along the beach as they ran back and forth chasing each other, stopping now and then to throw pebbles into the sea. I was by now carrying the shoes and socks (oh! the joys of parenthood). After a while they stopped and set about building a sandcastle. They worked busily away as I looked out across the sea and up towards the headland a short distance away. I could hear them muttering to each other. My daughter said, "You go for a walk Dad, we'll be okay on our own."

Sensing they wanted to be on their own to build the castle I said. "OK I will walk along the clifftop. How long shall I be."

"As long as you like, but at least an hour," she said.

So off I went, leaving them busily building their sandcastle, congenially discussing the project between them as they worked. It was quite blustery on the clifftop but not too cold. I glanced back occasionally, keeping them in sight. I sat for awhile on a bench then walked back timing my absence to an hour. As I drew close I could see they had finished building their sandcastle, and were sitting in the sand chatting. They noticed me approaching and rose to their feet smiles on their faces. I smiled back. They motioned towards their sandcastle. "What do you think of it Dad," asked my daughter.

I looked at the sandcastle. The sandcastle itself was not particularly impressive.They had no bucket and spade but had made do with their hands and stones to dig and build with. What was impressive to me was the amazing variety of stones of varying sizes, shapes and hues that they had gathered. Lacking the tools to build with they had formed a simple structure and had decorated it with these stones. They had wandered separately along the beach collecting stones, brought them back to their building site, and beautifully decorated their sandcastle with them. No arguments, no fighting and no sulking. Merely a sharing of ideas, and joint effort to accomplish the task they had set themselves.

"Its lovely. I like the way you have decorated it with the stones," I said. We smiled again at each other. "Lets go and get something to eat shall we," I said.

"Yeah! I'm starving," they both replied.

So off we went in search of a cafe. They walked either side of me contented, happily chatting.

What has all this to do with self defence you may ask? I believe that learning self defence should, if taught properly, teach children to work together developing their physical and mental skills. So that they will learn to exist within society together with others, some of whom may have greater or lesser skills in certain areas, without shame or an over developed sense of self importance. Leaning to work together with others for the good of society as a whole. Each taking pride in their own unique contribution, be it leader, organizer or humble worker. Cooperating together, each with respect for the other people and their contribution, without conflict.

I Fu Shou

I Fu Shou, also known as Sticky hand or Adhering Hand is an extremely important aspect of the Taoist arts. Sets and forms can be practised individually or in groups, and much can be understood about the self through the practice of these. The practice of I Fu Shou, however, can only be practised with a partner and through this tactile medium one can develop a depth of sensitivity that seems paranormal. To the uninitiated who try to explain it through the use of logic and physiology it is a maze of contradictions. Known in some parts of China as the Enlightened Hand, the dedicated practice of this art opens up the practitioner to their powers of heightened sensitivity. These palpable skills are developed through the dedicated practice of I Fu Shou over a long period of time. Slowly, by being in constant contact with your partner, you will be able to perceive which leg carries most of their weight. The weight may be on the ball of the foot, the heel, the little toe edge or the instep. You will also know instantly if your partner becomes tense at all in any part of their body.

To practise I Fu Shou you will need a partner to practise with. Having found a willing participant, you stand facing each other with the right foot ahead of the left. Both knees are bent slightly, with the body weight evenly distributed between both legs. The right foot is placed so that the instep of the right foot is close to but not touching the instep of your partner's right foot. Then the right hand is raised in front of the chest, so that when your partner does the same the back of your wrists lightly touch together. The body can move in any desired direction but the feet must remain stationary at all times. If you have to lift your toes or heel off the floor, or move either foot in any direction, then you are considered to have lost control of your balance. Later, when some skill has been developed, the students will move the feet, but only to set patterns as instructed. This training is only taught to advanced students.

The contact through the hands can be varied to any part of the arm, which includes the fingers, hand, all of the arm, the shoulder and the shoulder blade. Another rule is that contact must never be broken. You can slide the hand up and down your partner's arms or rotate round them, even change hands if you wish, although initially only one hand is usually used until you gain a little experience. When two hands are brought into play only one hand should be in contact at any one time, and if you wish to change hands, the second hand must always make contact before you remove the first so that contact is maintained throughout.

The object of the I Fu Shou exercise is to upset your partner's balance. This is not because it is a competition with a winner and a loser. Sadly, I see that 'pushing Hands competitions' are starting to appear, with some T'ai Chi Organizations subsequently advertising that one of their students won this or that section, presumably in the believe that this will attract more students to their organization. The type of students that this attracts are the ones who want to win competitions and show off in front of a crowd. I feel this is a retrograde step that moves away from the spirit of T'ai Chi. I do not consider that I Fu Shou should be presented as a form of competition which inevitably breeds a winner and a loser. I consider it to be a voyage of self discovery, the practise of which will enable the practitioner to develop a heightened state of awareness, firstly of themselves, then others they come into contact with. There is nothing to lose but your ego. And the prize to be won is humility.

Perhaps by looking at the names given to this exercise we can understand the different philosophy behind them. Firstly, to push.

This word is defined as meaning to exert force on a thing, to move away from oneself or from the origin of the force. This in essence seems rather an aggressive attitude. This type of philosophy leads to ambition, desire, glorification of the self and the wish to make oneself superior. This inevitably leads to separation from the Tao (way). There is no harmony here, only conflict. 'Sticky' is defined as: tending or intended to stick or adhere. Adhere is defined as: stick fast to a surface, another substance, etc. Also, to behave according to; follow in detail or give support or allegiance.

These words explain the essence of the instruction I have received from my master. He has always taught me that once contact has been made it must be maintained, and that this contact should be light, so light in fact, that if a feather were to fall upon your arm then the arm would sink under the weight of the feather. He also taught me that the object of the exercise was to follow the movements of your partner, not to force them to change the direction but to allow them to move their hand and arm in whatever way they wish. Learn to work within this framework whilst maintaining your own balance. Give in to their force which completely negates their strength and allows you to gently guide them in the direction they wish to go. Gently, help them on their way. If you offer no resistance, then no matter how much force is used against you, it cannot restrict your freedom. When you in to their force and offer no resistance, your partner sacrifices their balance when they exert force against your arm. By this action they create a weakness within their posture that can be exploited allowing you to maintain your balance whilst upsetting theirs.

The object of this is not to gain power over your partner, but to learn to remain in control of your own balance whilst being put under pressure by your partner. This helps us to deal with the problems we encounter in everyday life without losing control and resorting to violence. And by violence I do not necessarily mean physical violence but also mental violence, which is the modern way to bully and make people fear you. Power hungry people weave their webs of mental manipulation, preying on the weak within our society. We are all weak at some time or another as we fall into our yin periods during our journey through life. There are no laws that can be enforced effectively that will eradicate this kind of mental violence that we all have to suffer at some time or other at work, from parents, teachers and countless enthusiastic exponents of officialdom. We just have to learn to deal with it. We have to learn to take responsibility for ourselves. Instead of becoming physically or verbally violent, which can only escalate the conflict, we have to learn to absorb the energy thrown our way. In doing so we strengthen ourselves and weaken the perpetrator. More importantly, we remain entire.

Through the constant practice of I Fu Shou your partner learns that the amount of pressure they can safely exert is in direct relationship to their balance, and not their physical strength. I am sure you can see the value in knowing your limitations. This is what your partner learns from his position, and you have the opportunity to learn the lesson too when the roles are reversed. When your partner applies pressure to your wrist and you give in to this you must both maintain contact and as I mentioned earlier this must be light. As your partner slowly shifts his or her weight forward onto their front leg, they explore the limits of movement they have in this direction. They create muscle changes within their body as they move and with constant practice they will become aware of these muscle changes. They will also, after much practice, begin to feel any tension in their partner. If they do not move their weight forwards they do not explore their own limitations. However, if they push forwards too far and their partner does not resist but gives in correctly to their force, their balance will become unstable and their posture become weak. This is inevitable. If you want to learn how to keep your balance under pressure, you must first learn what it feels like to lose your balance. Or as my Master was fond of saying : "There are two sides to a coin. Look at both sides to understand it fully." If you have never allowed yourself willingly to be put under pressure to learn your own limitations the Tao (way) will do it for you. The practice of I Fu Shou should not be taken lightly, but it should be enjoyed. It should be taken seriously, but it should be indulged in, as if at play. Like life, it is a serious business, but I believe life is meant to be enjoyed also. There is so much beauty in nature and other people. Yet so many prefer to see only what is visible to the eye, accepting what they see without question, never looking any deeper. There is an old Chinese saying : " You cannot tell how deep a pool is by looking at it." You must jump in to see for yourself. Most people wear a mask. This they present to the world, afraid to show their true selves, for in doing so they know they will become vulnerable, and from this they hide. You need to look beneath the surface to see the real person.

If you continue to resist force with force your life will be one long struggle. You will endure constant conflict, day after day until you start to look inwards at yourself and stop blaming others for your constant misfortune. You must learn to take responsibility for yourself. Learn to look after yourself when life gets difficult by remaining entire. Learn to give in to forces that are greater than you, for you will only damage yourself by opposing them, creating more and more conflict in the process. Instead of looking only outwards at others faults, look inwards and explore your own imbalance, learn to recognize your own weaknesses and your own inner conflict. However, if you have the courage to look within, to recognize your own shortcomings, then, and only then, can you start to eradicate them. Make no mistake, this takes real courage. If you persist in the illusion that you are perfect and everyone else is against you, your life will be one long miserable existence full of conflict. Those who would like to help others to make the world a better place must first learn to make themselves a better person.

Once they have accomplished this task, helping others will be a natural progression. If they have not learnt to govern themselves first any help they offer to others or any contribution they make to the government of the world will only add to the chaos. Can a blind man show others how to see properly?

I believe that within the practice of T'ai Chi all the lessons of life are contained. And I practise it with as much fervour as I can muster. I have learnt much from my practice of T'ai Chi, but there is much, much more to learn. And the more I practise the more eager I become. For me, it is like a passionate love affair. And just as when one is in love the world seems a truly beautiful place, so to me the world with all its problems is still a beautiful place. The natural world in all its beauty and diversity was created by God. The problems are created by man's greed, always wanting more and more, never satisfied. Unable to see the beauty in nature he constantly seeks to please the senses. This pleasing of the senses is short-lived and therefore must constantly be sought after. This leads inevitably to greed. My Master has always taught me that the yin comes before the yang. In other words you must give before your can receive. In serving others you serve yourself. Look after your car, make sure it has enough oil, water and fuel, and it will serve you well. Try to save money by denying it oil and it will continue to run, providing you replenish its fuel tank. But it is false economy because the lack of oil will cause problems to the engine, the heart of the car. Before very long it will break down and cost a lot of money and time to repair. So, if you really value your car, care for it properly and it will serve you well. So it is with our planet. If we pollute the water and the air whilst raping the earth of its treasures, concerned only with our material development, either blind or just too greedy to care about the damage we are doing to the Earth's ecosystem, we will slowly be annihilating ourselves.

The same lessons are learned from I Fu Shou. When you practise I Fu Shou with your partner, your partner acts as a mirror image for you. Where you can see and feel their ambition and desire exposed in their will to win as they try to upset your balance you see your own ambitions and desire to accomplish reflected before you. By learning to deny your own ambition and desires you begin to see the futility of your partner's wish to accomplish a goal that is, upset your balance. By not responding to their force with force you will learn to gently guide your partner whilst remaining in control of your own balance. Please note that you gently guide, not push or force him, off balance, so that he may see the futility of his ambition and desire, so that he may see that by your gentle and unresisting nature that it is his own force without any consideration as to the effect it will have on his balance that causes him to lose his equilibrium. Blinded by his own ambition and desire he loses awareness of his own physical body. To separate yourself in this way is to separate yourself from the Tao (way). For your physical body is the vehicle you have been given to make the journey through life. It needs to be kept in good working order, and it must be under your complete control, for taking a journey in a vehicle that is out of control is folly. This jewel (your body) given to you by the supreme spirit should be cared for as best you can. If you gave someone the most precious gift you could possibly give them because you loved them so dearly, and if your loved one did not take care of your precious gift, would this not upset you?

Plunge your hand into water and the water gives way to accept the intrusion. Remove your hand and the water fills the space it occupied immediately. There is no space where your hand was and no evidence that it ever existed in that space. The important thing to remember is that it is the work you do in service to others whilst you live that is important. Once you depart this life you will be quickly forgotten.

The contact made with the earth through the feet is a very important aspect of I Fu shou. There are many reasons for this and they incorporate the physical, mental and spiritual. On a physical level it can be easily seen that if the contact with the ground is not good then the balance is obviously not going to be very stable. So we must use the mental faculties to keep trace of our balance which is dependent on the contact our feet have with the floor. If we lose our mental concentration, however briefly, we lose awareness of that contact our feet have with the floor and therefore our balance is easily upset.

Through the practice of I Fu Shou on a spiritual level we are reminded that every time we give the brain complete autonomy it ignores the information given through the senses. It ignores the information given on the state of balance transferred from the feet. The brain now in complete control ignores the subtle changes in posture, movements of the joints and muscle changes within the body. The brain considers these purely automatic and merely a reaction to existing conditions. The brain is like a child that bullies others, given control usually either through fear, complacency or laziness, it takes over and looking to the future makes a judgement on what it wants to happen. After an analytical appraisal of existing conditions, the brain makes its calculation and then commands the body to obey its instructions. The problem here is that the brain is working on information which is now based on the past and at best was only partial, omitting as it did the subtle information available through the senses. The brain has also made calculations as to a future event, it considers this event, an inevitable conclusion based on its analysis of the situation. The only thing that has not entered the equation is the only thing that really matters, THE PRESENT.

Spiritually the only thing that matters is the present. To be able to live in the present totally is the aim of all those who aspire to follow the Tao (way). To be able to live moment to moment is the only way to learn the truth. The truth is all around us constantly, it is there for all to see. It is hidden from no one. Yet very few ever see it, for they persist in looking for it in the past, or searching for it in the future which has not yet been born. The truth is in the present and you must reach it through an understanding of yourself. If you do not understand who you are, how can you understand where you are? And if you do not understand where you are, how can you ever hope to understand the ever changing conditions that surround you? Maintaining an awareness of the contact our feet have with the floor during our I Fu Shou practice. is akin to the realization that our experiences, through the medium of our physical bodies whilst our feet are firmly planted on mother earth, are all we have. If we lose contact with our own physical presence now, we cease to be. We are asleep. If we lose this contact and allow the brain to enter into a world of illusion that it creates through its analysis of the past, which is gone forever, then we lose contact with reality. For we are here on this earth, in this physical body, experiencing these sensations through the senses. This is how we learn. Not the learning of mathematics, physics, history. The type of learning we are discussing here is researching of the self. Instead of looking outwards, we look inwards at ourselves. We recognize our own desires, ambitions, fears and the aggression we use in an effort to obtain what we want. We learn through the practice of I Fu Shou, and other sections of T'ai Chi, to recognize these in ourselves first. And the practice of I fu shou is particularly useful, working as we do with a partner who acts as a mirror image of ourselves for us, reflecting the desire, ambition, fear and the aggression we all have within us.

The first step is recognizing that if these negative qualities exist in others, then they must surely exist in us also. We cannot deal with something that we refuse to admit exists. If we deny our own desire, ambition, fear and aggression how are we to learn how to bring these under control? One must have the courage to make oneself vulnerable. To look at oneself clearly and see the work that needs to be done to improve the self. Have the courage to suffer the humiliation that will be heaped upon your shoulders by those who consider themselves without fault. In the eyes of some you will be weak, but if you persist, out of this weakness will be born strength, as surely as day follows night. 'The Meek Shall Inherit The Earth.' And when you gain this strength, remember the road you travelled to get there. Be tolerant of others as you pass them along the road. If they laugh at you or swear and curse you, be tolerant, for as Jesus said, `Forgive them, for they know not what they do.' On your path you will meet many sceptics along the road. You will pass them, occasionally one at a time, and at other times you will encounter groups of them, but your inner strength will sustain you. You will pass them not because you are travelling faster than they are. You will pass them because you are going the other way down the road in the opposite direction to them. Whilst they travel outwards seeking new and greater experiences with which to please their senses, you will be travelling inwards.

The truth is within yourself. So look inside yourself do not be afraid. Find out who the real you is. Then you can start to follow you own true path in life which is your own personal Tao (way). Be warned! You must be prepared to encounter many travellers going in the opposite direction, many of whom will mock and curse you, but among them will be some who will recognize the peace, serenity, love of mankind and the love for all God's creatures that you are trying to cultivate. Some will listen to your advice, some will scorn it. Accept both! Be grateful for the opportunity to help some, and have pity for those that are not able to see the truth. We must never judge others because we do not know their path. We are only human not divine, and therefore our under-standing is always limited. So suffer the scorn and accept the thanks. The yin and yang exists in everything.

When we train in the discipline of I Fu Shou we are developing sensitivity. This training has a depth that like the Tao is infinite. It is a fascinating journey of self discovery. We start by looking at ourselves. Through the practice of I Fu Shou we slowly become aware of our subtle muscular changes as we transfer our weight from one leg to the other. We become aware of our weight distribution on each foot and exactly where on the foot most of the weight is, the ball of the foot, the heel, the instep or the little toe edge. The mind is brought under control and made aware of the body's subtle movements. In this way the physical body and the mind are harmonized. When we are familiar with our own movements and are able to harmonize the body and mind we can then concentrate on paying attention to the movements our partners are making, learning to respond to these movements, rather than control our own movements whilst endeavouring to control theirs at the same time, and simultaneously attempting to upset their balance.

Let us look at the above paragraph and expand on it a little. If we try simultaneously to control our own movements, whilst analysing our partner's, then calculating the reaction, proceed to execute the necessary action to upset our partner's balance. Is this not an impossible task? Indeed it is. What has happened here is that we have allowed the brain to take control. The brain is considered sacrosanct in the western world. It is revered, considered supreme over our other human attributes. It is not! It is a tool that has great use, but it is only a tool like the many other attributes that we have at our disposal. And we must learn to harmonize them for greatest efficiency. For, like the fingers on our hands, each finger is separate in its own right, but it is still part of the hand. And while each finger can operate separately, it must harmonize with the others to make the hand useful. Given complete autonomy the brain darts from one thought to another, completely out of control, just like the unruly child who will not harmonize with those around it, but seeks to control by creating chaos. The brain, like the unruly child, must be disciplined and made to harmonize with the body's other attributes. Otherwise we are like the car driver who takes a car out on the open road without having learnt how to control it first. With some difficulty we start the car, manage to get it into gear and hurtle off down the road to the noise of crunching gears and screeching tires. We have thought about where we want to go. We look eagerly at the road ahead as we hurtle along. Devoid of authority over the cars controls, we career downhill, a danger to ourselves and all others in our path. If we want to learn to drive properly we must seek the instruction of another who has the skill and ability to teach us properly. So it is with I Fu Shou and the other sections of T'ai Chi. One needs the instruction of a skilled practitioner, if one is to proceed down the right path. These things cannot be learnt from a book, because a book can only teach you on a very superficial level. Only a teacher who has travelled the road can instruct you properly. Otherwise you will travel many miles down the wrong road before realizing that the wrong path has been taken. Training with a partner who also has not had correct instruction is like the blind leading the blind.

So where does one find a teacher? It is said that : 'When the student is ready the master will appear.' Many people consider themselves ready for spiritual training and go in search of a teacher. They may travel the whole world seeking the ultimate teacher only to find that they must start at the beginning, with themselves. Then, when the Tao sees that you are a conscientious and serious seeker of truth, a teacher will appear and be seen for who he is. One must empty one's mind to see and hear clearly. If one's mind is full of ambition greed and desire it will inevitable colour what one sees and hears, it will inevitably blind one to the truth. If you are unable to see yourself for who you are you will be unable to recognize a real teacher should you meet one. There is a story that once there was a man who had studied with all the various teachers in his area, he had studied all the books he could find in his pursuit of knowledge. One day a traveller told him of a town that he had visited that was renowned for the many spiritual masters that lived there. These men it was said had knowledge that was unsurpassed. The man decided he would go there and seek out one of these masters to further his knowledge. He arrived there about midday and made enquiries as to the whereabouts of the masters, but as no-one seemed to be able to help him, he concluded that these people were simple minded people who knew nothing of the masters. Obviously he would have to search out the masters himself. These simpletons would be of no help at all. All day he searched to no avail. Late in the evening, tired and weary, but determined to succeed he came upon an elderly man, who just having left a house nearby was struggling to lift his motorbike that had blown over in the wind. The man passed by, his mind consumed with his search. As he passed the elderly man called out to him. 'Excuse me, he said, you seem a strong young man, could you lift my motorbike up for me please.'

'No,' replied the man, impatient to be on his way.

'Why not?' asked the elderly man.

'It is to heavy for me,' replied the man.

'Would you please try? I am too weak on my own and I need to be on my way. I am the local plumber and I have another call to make,' asked the elderly man.

'There is no point. I have told you I cannot lift it. it would be a waste of time,' replied the man.

'How do you know you cannot lift it if you have not tried?' asked the elderly man.

'I cannot stand here wasting my time arguing with you,' said the man rudely. 'I am too busy.'

And off he went to continue his search. After a few days he gave up his search and went home. He concluded that the traveller had either not told him the truth or that the masters became tired of being surrounded by such simpletons and had moved elsewhere. His obsession with himself and his own ambitions, greed and desires robbed him of his love and compassion for his fellow man and blinded him to the wisdom in the elderly plumber's words. He had met a master but failed to recognize him. Work on yourself. Purge yourself. And when a master passes your way you will see him for who he is, not what you think he should be.

The benefits to be gained from the practice of I Fu Shou are many and varied. On a physical level, the constant weight distribution from one leg to the other will tone up the muscular system, improve posture and increase flexibility. The concentration required to monitor the body's movement develops a disciplined mind capable of dynamic control over the body. This control over the body is not the contrived conclusion of the brain's analysis. No, this dynamic control is born out of the mind's sensitivity, its total awareness of the body's state of being - right now - and its ever constant movement. The body is always in constant movement, like everything else in nature. Just the very act of breathing sets the body swaying and the balance must be constantly monitored and adjusted because of this. It fact, if you want to prove this to yourself, you can - right now - all you have to do is stand up, relax and breathe. As you breathe, try to stay relaxed and feel the constant movement and adjustment that your body makes. Interesting isn't it? Or did you just read it, taking my word for it? To know the truth you have to do it yourself. Then and only then will you have learnt the truth of the matter. But you must do the exercise with an open mind, not start with any preconceived conclusions produced by the brain. If you feel nothing, then you have just proved how out of touch you are with your own body. Modern life is making you too tense. Seek out a class which teaches relaxation, preferably a T'ai Chi Class in your area, in the absence of which, any class that teaches relaxation, such as yoga, will help. Don't think, 'I will do it next week.' Do it now. Start to redress the balance, start to reduce the stress modern life places on us all, but do it now, because tomorrow never gets here.

Most people are neither aware nor interested in understanding their physical selves in this way. That is their choice and who am I to say they are wrong? But, for those who wish to follow a spiritual path and be of service to others then these things are of paramount importance, because the way to the spirit is through an understanding of the self. And this is precisely what I Fu Shou is all about. The appreciation and depth of understanding of the world we live in that follows will open the dedicated student's eyes to the fact that even with all the problems and violence that are prevalent in society today, there is much beauty to behold, if only you can let go of your own desires, ambition and therefore conflict so that it can be seen:

"IT IS ONLY WITH THE HEART THAT ONE CAN SEE RIGHTLY.

WHAT IS ESSENTIAL IS INVISIBLE TO THE EYE."

Diet

The question of which diet is healthier, one including meat or one excluding meat (commonly referred to as a vegetarian diet), has been argued over the years, with the supporters of eating meat by far outnumbering the vegetarians. I myself follow the Taoist long life diet 'Chang Ming' which differs somewhat from a vegetarian diet. However, it shares with a vegetarian diet what to my mind is the most important ingredient of any diet, the total exclusion of red meat. I am firmly convinced that abstaining from eating red meat is a more natural diet for human beings.

The word 'vegetarian' is not derived from 'vegetable' as most people think, but from the Latin word 'vegus' which means "full of life". Some of the world's greatest thinkers abstained from meat, among them: Leonardo Da Vinci, Sir Isaac Newton, St. Francis of Assisi and Albert Einstein, who said: "It is my view that the vegetarian manner of living, by its purely physical effect on the human temperament would most beneficially influence the lot of mankind."

Pythagoras, who is generally given credit for its inception, praised vegetarianism for its hygienic nature and the kinship it fostered between man and the animals. In the past, most doctors, nutritionists and those responsible for health education, have in the main stated that a diet which contained no meat could not be healthy because this kind of diet would be lacking in certain minerals and vitamins, especially the B group of vitamins. In recent years the trend towards eating less meat has increased because the technology that has so successfully increased meat production is an unnatural method. The use of chemicals and the unnatural living conditions the animals are kept in, which in many cases are appalling, are designed to force growth. People are now becoming increasingly concerned about their intake of chemicals and fat via the food chain. Some scientists believe that the chemicals fed to these animals will lead to an accelerated ageing in humans. We are constantly told by our doctors that we must reduce our fat intake to lower cholesterol levels. No food from the plant world contains cholesterol. Using modern technology, nutritionists have shown that the body can obtain all it requires to remain healthy without eating meat. Many people now consider it wrong to kill animals for food when this is not necessary for survival. Perhaps they feel as Leonardo Da Vinci did when he said, "I have from an early age forsworn the use of meat, and the time will come when men will look upon the slaughter of animals as they now look upon the slaughter of men."

The International Development Research Centre in Ottawa claims: "Meat production in western countries is cheating the rest of the world of much-needed food." In view of this, eating meat is a wanton waste of resources. The amount of food an animal eats is out of all proportion to the amount of edible meat it produces. In fact, the modern battery chicken, which is the most efficient in converting its food to flesh, takes around 12lbs of food to produce 1lb of meat (not including the bones). Pigs eat 20lbs and cows 30lbs of food to produce one pound of meat. Sheep usually graze on land that is unsuitable for crops and they are fortunate enough to roam free, at least until market day. Every pound of food that is grown for feeding to animals to produce eating meat is a pound of food less for a person. So while we indulge ourselves in eating meat, others must go hungry. Still, we can always send our old clothes and perhaps an old blanket or two via Oxfam to ease our consciences, perhaps even give a little of our hard earned cash. But while we try to cure the symptoms instead of the cause, hoping the problem will go away or somebody else will sort it out, more people starve to death. But we are not really interested in tackling the cause because it would involve altering our eating habits and we must have our meat. Our selfish greed robs us of our affection and compassion for our fellow man.

Scientific research has shown that children born to vegetarian mothers are as healthy as babies born to omnivorous mothers. Still-birth, premature deliveries and birth defects occur no more or less frequently in vegetarian women than in any other particular group. The strongest animals who possess the greatest endurance, the horse, the ox, the elephant, are all vegetarians, as are many of our world class sports people. The physical apparatus of humans is not like that of a natural carnivore, which has sharp teeth and claws for tearing flesh. Our teeth resemble more closely the vegetarian animals who have flat molars for grinding. Furthermore, carnivores have short intestines, usually no more then three times the length of the trunk, so that meat can be quickly eliminated from the body before it has had time to putrefy. Human intestines are huge, up to 12 times the length of the body, giving the meat plenty of time to turn rank inside the intestinal tract and poison the consumer.

Social conditioning plays an enormous part in our eating habits. For instance, the thought of eating steak and kidney pie for breakfast may seem ridiculous, yet three hours later it is welcomed. Food snobbery is in evidence when foods like caviar and pheasant are valued not because they are more nutritious foods, but because they cost more or are associated with the upper classes. Food advertisers play on our emotions by conjuring up pleasant memories or confirming social images associated with the consumption of their products, all in an effort to sell more. We must resist these temptations for the good of our health.

The Irish Playwright George Bernard Shaw, himself a vegetarian, was once very ill. His doctors warned him that unless he began to eat eggs and drink a broth made with a meat base, he would die.

Rather than heed the doctors' advice, Shaw called for his private secretary. In the doctors' presence Shaw dictated his final instructions: 'I solemnly declare that it is my last wish that when I am no longer a captive of this physical body, that my coffin when carried to the graveyard be accompanied by mourners of the following categories: first, birds; second, sheep, lambs, cows, and other animals of the kind; third, live fish in an aquarium. Each of these mourners should carry a placard bearing the inscription: 'O lord, be gracious to our benefactor George Bernard Shaw who gave his life for saving ours!' George Bernard Shaw also once said, "Mankind will never have peace until we stop killing and eating animals." I believe this to be true. For if we cannot show animals love and respect, allowing them to live out their lives naturally, I do not see how we can ever truly learn to love and respect each other. If this is so then we shall never end the conflict and misery that we impose upon one another in our continual struggle for personal prosperity. If we are to live together in peace and co-operation we must first stop eating meat.

Many foods that have beneficial qualities also contain properties that are not good for the human body. Meat, which contains many minerals and proteins, also introduces large amounts of cholesterol, high concentrations of which is believed to accelerate arteriosclerosis. Many packaged foods in our supermarkets contain large amounts of sugar which pollute the taste buds masking the true flavour of the food. Our taste buds are educated to expect this sweet pleasurable taste in everything we eat. Our bodies become hooked on sugar and eventually most foods not containing sugar are considered awful in taste and are therefore shunned. Excessive sugar consumption is just as addictive as alcohol, nicotine and caffeine. These substances harm the consumer's health in the long run. Caffeine is very addictive and when combined with large amounts of sugar, as it is in many canned drinks, is extremely detrimental to the future health of our children. Caffeine is an alkaloid drug, and we should discourage its use by our young children so that they do not grow up dependent on their daily intake to function effectively. This I believe is a very serious matter. In the affluent western world, we are in great danger of becoming, if we are not already, dependent on our daily intake of these drugs. No wonder we pay scant attention to the natural world and our destruction of the earth's resources. We are becoming like the drug addict who will do anything to pay for his next fix. Like these poor souls driven out of their minds by a craving they cannot control, we seek only to please the senses by obtaining more and more possessions and experiences. And most of us are prepared to turn a blind eye to the suffering that is incurred in the process.

The food we eat is of vital importance to our health, both physically and mentally, and therefore spiritually. I will end this chapter with a quote from the 'Tao Te Chin' that great Chinese classical work. If you have not read this book I strongly recommend you do. The wisdom contained within its pages is as relevant today as it was in ancient China when in was written. I quote from The Richard Wilhelm edition which is the translation that is my personal preference. The text of this book is divided into two main parts. The second part entitled 'Life' (DE) and I quote the first few lines from section 38

Whosoever cherishes life does not know about life
therefore he has life.

Whosoever does not cherish life seeks not to lose life:
therefore he has no life.

My interpretation of this in relation to diet is that if you live only to eat and are intoxicated by the pleasures of food, your health, physically, mentally and spiritually, will not develop correctly. Your perception of the world and conditions surrounding you will be severely coloured by your addiction to the pleasures of eating.

If you eat to live, there is still pleasure in the consumption of your food but without the excessive addiction. The body will be nourished adequately without having to deal with excesses that are a burden on the physical system. The mind will be freer from the constraint of the body's addiction and able to appreciate the realities of the world and its surroundings to a larger degree. The greater harmony of body and mind will ensure that the purification of the spirit is not unnecessarily hindered.

Finally, an ascetic approach to diet in my opinion is also incorrect. Food is provided by God that we may nourish our bodies and replenish our energies. I believe we should enjoy these gifts and give thanks. We should eat to live and not over indulge or waste food. If we over indulge and waste food while others go hungry elsewhere, rear animals for food in unnatural and restrictive conditions, how can man's spirit become free to soar to new heights? Much more could be said about diet but I think this will suffice for the present. You may agree or disagree with the opinions I have expressed here. You must make up your own mind, take responsibility for your own diet. After all if you lived in Iceland or were part of the nomadic Bedouin people it would be rather difficult if not impossible to comply with the suggestions made here.

Love

First let me make it clear that I do not pretend to know what love in its purist form is. I do know however from my own experience that my concept of love has changed as I have grown and developed. So please understand that the following opinion is based on my present limited understanding. There are of course many kinds of love, love of a friend, love of one's child, love of a parent, the love between man and woman, love of ones job. Then there is the love of God, the supreme spirit. This is the most important love of all and the others pale in its presence. Without this love of God - or whatever name you prefer to use for the supreme spirit - all the other kinds of love are meaningless and false, based on greed, power, ambition, desire and the propping up of one's ego which inevitably leads to a lack of pride in oneself and one's existence, which leads back to a need to bolster the ego again. Round and round we go in this endless circle, seeking more and more outwards expressions of love. We become like the hamster on its treadwheel, racing forwards faster and faster until exhaustion causes it to stop and rest. But then like the hamster, once rested, up we jump, we get back on the treadmill again to expend all our energy getting nowhere.

People look for the source of rivers by travelling against the flow. The further they travel in this direction the smaller the river becomes until eventually it is only a trickle coming out of the ground on the side of a mountain. If on the other hand they had travelled with the flow, instead of against, it they would have expended much less energy. They would have found the river became bigger and bigger, full of exciting discoveries. The further one is able to travel with the flow the bigger the river becomes until eventually it joins the sea, the source of all life on earth. This source of all ephemeral life is provided by the Tao (God) so that we may be nourished and prosper. The sea, like the Tao, has a depth that is beyond our understanding. Learn to travel with the flow and life becomes a constant source of knowledge which is ever expanding; travel against the flow and life becomes restrictive and true knowledge scarce.

The way to find true love is to look within yourself. Examine yourself, look at your habits, at work and at home amongst your family. Watch other people and their reactions to you. Instead of blaming others for any problems and misunderstandings, examine your own part in things. Could you have perhaps explained yourself better? If you had paid more attention to the other people you were dealing with perhaps you would have noticed their confusion. Learn to care for people, not pretend to care, but REALLY care. By looking at yourself in this way, watching others reactions to you, other people become a mirror image of yourself. As you learn to behave better towards others, you will learn to be proud of yourself, to love yourself. You must start with yourself because you cannot possible learn to love others without having first learnt to love yourself. This love comes from within and radiates outwards. If you learn to really care for and love others, then they in turn will eventually learn to care for and love you. You cannot first receive gifts of love, only then giving back in return. YOU must give before you can receive, and it is not possible to give to others that which you yourself do not possess.

If you will start to observe yourself, to look inwards, you can put yourself in contact with the Tao (God, The Supreme Spirit), the source of all things. Once you have done this, providing your intentions are pure, you will receive an input of loving energy which will assist you in your task. Once you have learnt to love yourself it will be a natural progression for you to want to love and care for others to repay the gift you were given. As you give love and care in whatever way you can to others, you will receive more gifts from the supreme spirit, some directly, some through the deeds of others. You can never repay this debt because the love of the supreme spirit is unlimited and we poor wretched mortals cannot possibly ever come close to matching it. Be grateful and give thanks to the supreme spirit in your prayers and through doing good deeds for others.

Friends, true friends, are hard to find these days, as most people are too busy trying to make themselves materially more prosperous to develop real friendships. A loyal friend is a rare and precious thing indeed. If we want a friend ourselves, then instead of complaining that we do not have one, the answer is to become a good, loyal friend to someone else. If we become a good, loyal friend to someone else, we will in turn have a good, loyal friend ourselves. We must give in order to receive.

Loving our children is taken for granted, but many parents certainly do not love their children. The constant stream of cases of child abuse and the misbehaviour of our youth at home and abroad at football matches and the like prove this. We are not accepting responsibility for our children, not teaching them the spiritual values necessary for them to develop into mature sensible adults. Instead we blame the government and education authorities for the problems. Children who lack self discipline have often learnt this from their elders and are allowed to behave this way at home. When God gave you the gift of a child to love and nurture and you accepted this gift, you accepted the responsibility that goes with it, to do your best to educate your child how to be a good useful human being. And in doing so you must accept the suffering that loving and caring for your child will bring. The sleepless nights. The feeling of total helplessness when your lovely tiny pink bundle of joy gets sick or is teething, and you can only watch, unable to take away their pain which you would gladly do if you were able. Yes, you will certainly experience much pain in your efforts to bring up your child, but you will also be rewarded with many moments of great joy.

Love, true love that is, is a state beyond pain and pleasure. Pain and pleasure are like the Yin and Yang aspect of love. One goes with the other, each an opposite yet complementary component of the whole. I repeat that I do not claim to understand completely what love is. But I do know! I know that love is not pleasure alone. As best as I can ascertain, love is the total acceptance of these two composite factors without becoming either melancholy when confronted with suffering in the course of love, or becoming unduly euphoric when experiencing the pleasures of love. For the pleasures that love can bring are gifts given, not prizes won. The pain and pleasure that love brings should not be suppressed but neither should it be allowed to consume you.

The love for a parent is something which tends to change in its nature as we grow into adults. As children we love our parents because they provide for us, feed us, clothe us and give us advice which helps us to deal with the world around us. Psychology tells us that the greatest, usually unconscious, fear most children have is that they will be abandoned by their parents and left to fend for themselves. So as children we have a primal instinct to stick close to our parents. Parents naturally nurture their offspring, this is the way of nature and is seen throughout the animal kingdom. As we grow older and wiser we strike out more and more on our own. Often this is a difficult time for both parents and children alike. Parents are inclined to make rules for behaviour which are based on conditions prevalent during the same period in their childhood. Their children consider these restrictions unreasonable.

We live in a world where changes take place much faster then they ever have previously. Out great grandparents lived in an era when life changed very little from one generation to another. They lived out their lives mostly in farming communities where sons followed their fathers, doing the same work as their fathers and then in turn passing on these skills to their own sons. Everyone lived in closely-knit groups and hardly ever travelled far from the community in which they lived.

Our own parents lived in an era during which enormous changes took place in industry. Whole industries either changed radically or completely disappeared leaving people out of work. These people had to be retrained in other skills which were in short supply or in the new skills required for the new industries that sprang up. The world was a new and exciting place for the young, with opportunities to do new and exciting things. But for their parents it was a very difficult time, when changes to the very fabric of their lives had to be made. No longer could a man leave school, start work in some local industry and expect to keep the same job for life as his father had. These new changes to life, as they always are, were quickly adopted by the young who, unlike their parents, were not hampered by the past which influenced their expectations of the future. Parents no longer understood the changing attitudes of their children and their children could not understand why their parents tried to impose standards of behaviour on them which did not match the conditions of the times. The closeness of the family unit and the close-knit communities began to break down. Friends and their families moved away to other areas, where new industries had sprung up, to find work. Sons and daughters left home to find employment elsewhere as local industries declined. So, separated by their differing attitudes and in some cases long distances from their children, parents became more resentful of their children's independence. Confused by the world around them, which was changing beyond recognition, and not being able to communicate effectively with their children inevitably led to a lack of respect from the children for their parents. The parents, in many cases, often either gave up communicating to the children in any meaningful way or became authoritarian in their attitudes, imposing their ideas by force.

The children having no guidance, at least none that was as far as they could see, relevant to the changing conditions that they were experiencing, made their own decisions based on their knowledge of the new world, which it has to be said was often superior to that of their parents. But these decisions were made without much experience of the social skills needed. The children ignored the advice of their parents which was rich in social skills developed from years of experience in close-knit family units. So the family unit of the past has changed forever.

Now, another generation later, a new relationship is developing between parents and their children. A relationship where parents are learning to accept the many continual changes that are constantly affecting their lives and those of their children, learning to allow their children more freedom and individuality with which to express themselves. In turn their children are learning to have more respect for their parents and listen to the advice they offer, then to take that advice, adding it to their own more modern understanding of the world, and then to make better and more balanced decisions concerning themselves and the environment around them.

Our children will inherit the wonders of the modern world. They will also inherit the problems we inadvertently created. Through living in closely-knit communities and caring only for the survival of our own group or country we have committed acts that were greedy and aggressive, preying on the weaknesses of other groups or countries so that ours may become more and more prosperous. The world and its people must now learn to live in harmony, together, caring for each other. For the world to survive we must look to the problems of the world as a whole unit, learning to respect each other's cultures. But the overriding concern must be the survival of the planet as a whole. We cannot chop down the rain forest without affecting, in the long term, our own environment. Yet we must understand the local people's needs. If their only means of feeding themselves now is by allowing the forest to be cut down and sold, we must understand that they are concerned with their immediate survival. They have no future if they cannot eat now.

Some months ago I watched a programme about the slaughter of the rhinoceros in Africa. As part of the programme they interviewed a poacher who had been caught and imprisoned. He was asked various questions about how many rhinoceros he had killed, how many poachers were in his group and how much they were paid for the horns. These wonderful animals are in danger of becoming extinct because the horns of the rhinoceros are prized for various reasons in different cultures. The poacher was then asked why he wished to have what to him was a very large amount of money. He replied that there was something that was very important to him and he wished to purchase one. At this point I was thinking to myself what a despicable man this was, how could anyone slaughter and risk the extinction of these beautiful creatures for mere financial gain? I thought he most probably wished to buy a shiny new BMW or some other fancy car to impress his friends with, or perhaps he wished to buy a grand house to live in. When he finally answered, I was stunned! He said he wanted to buy a grinding machine. This man's dream, was to be able to grind corn for others and thereby provide himself with legal employment and a prestigious and respected place in the community.

We are all children of God and we must, all learn to care for and appreciate all that he has provided for us. Not just the environment.

Not just the animal kingdom. Not just the people of other cultures. We must care for all three simultaneously because each depends on the other for its continuing existence. The animals, insects and birds condition the environment, the environment conditions us and the way we live. If we destroy either, in the long term, we destroy ourselves. If we are committed to loving our fellow man we can still keep our separate cultures and way of life, providing we can learn to tolerate each other's differences. The overriding factor must be the harmonizing of the planet's resources, so that all people have water that is drinkable and not polluted, food that is nourishing and not full of harmful chemicals. The animal kingdom, the environment and the people of the earth, all living in harmony. Maybe I am just a dreamer. But I believe it can be done; if we ALL WORK to make it happen. I believe the hope for the future lies in our children. We must do our utmost to pass on to them the lessons learnt from the past. Rekindle spiritual values so that compassion and love reign over greed and hate.

Much has been written about the love between man and woman by writers much more eminent than myself. However, I cannot ignore the subject and as I have recently found love myself, perhaps you will find my perspective interesting and I hope, thought provoking. In relation to Taoist philosophy, man is Yang and woman Yin. This must not be taken to mean that man is superior to woman. As I explained in the chapter on the Yin and Yang, these two composite factors emanate from the Tao and are the opposing, yet complimentary, principles from which all else manifests. Without the joining together of man and woman life cannot continue. Neither is superior to the other but at certain times each has more influence over the other depending on the conditions that are prevalent. To function correctly man and woman must harmonize together, supporting each other's weaknesses with their strengths.

Unfortunately, the image portrayed to us through magazines, films and advertisements on television and other media is one in which the man is a powerful figure who always wins by whatever means necessary. This man is admired and sought after by all the attractive females whom he then treats badly and they have constant arguments and fights. Making yourself rich and powerful at the expense of others is considered clever. The attractive, intelligent, modern woman is shown to be an assertive person (to the point of being aggressive) who manages to outsmart the men in her life and succeed in getting her way by manipulation. Is it any wonder that there are more and more families breaking up? Now I am of course aware that there are many more contributing factors in the increasing number of family separations. But not many people can live up to the image accepted as the ideal, therefore they feel inadequate and either become very passive or aggressive, neither of which is conducive to a balanced happy relationship. The image portrayed by the media is destructive and the more magazines, television and videos we watch that portray these images, the more we, and our children, are affected by it.

I believe that man and woman should complement each other. As a left and right hand is each separate in its own right, each capable of performing many tasks successfully. Yet each is limited. When they work together they expand their horizons beyond their wildest dreams. Once they have learnt to harmonize their strengths and weaknesses the daily toils of existence becomes easier. When a job needs to be done that is more suited to the right hand instead of the left hand struggling to perform this task, the right hand can with its more adequate skills complete the job with less effort. The left hand has been able to rest and observe its partner the right hand complete the job efficiently. Instead of depleting its energies struggling with a task unsuited to its capabilities, the left hand has conserved its energies, observed and learnt and, perhaps more importantly, the left hand, when called upon to do a task that is suitable to its abilities, will be fresh and have ample energy for the job. The right hand can now rest and observe. Working together they can complement or oppose each other; the choice is theirs. Man and woman, being Yang and Yin, can oppose or complement each other. Should they choose to oppose each other their lives will be full of conflict. If however they choose to complement each other, help each other over their difficulties and weaknesses, share in each other's successes and strengths, they can enjoy the serenity and happiness that the Tao (supreme spirit) wishes for them. This is the harmony of the Yin and Yang. Two complementary forces working together for the good of the whole.

I mentioned earlier that I have recently fallen in love myself with a wonderful woman who is a person I respect and admire, and when I am separated from her yearn for her company. It is as if I have always known her. I have known her for less than a year yet I feel I have known her all my life. Shortly after I met her I was inspired to write her a poem. I have never written a poem before. It came from I don't know where and after I had finished I realized that with a slight alteration it would express my sentiment for the Tao or God. Primarily however it was written to express my feeling for this lovely lady the Tao has sent me to share my life with. I have never felt so completely compatible, so much admiration, so much respect and so much in love ever before. Before meeting this lady I thought I knew what love was. Now I know love is more than I previously thought. When I first met her I felt I loved her completely and it was not possible to love more. Yet the more I know her the more I find myself loving her. I never knew love like this existed and it just keeps growing. As an aspiring Taoist I should have known better because the Tao (God) is unlimited and therefore love also is unlimited. When I say my prayers I thank the Lord for this gift. I don't know what I did to deserve such a gift but I am truly grateful. This is love, the like of which, until now, I have never known.

Atheists argue that the existence of sin and chaos in the world is evidence of Gods' non-existence. Why is there sin and chaos in the world? Why does God allow these things to happen? As a believer in a supreme spirit (God), I have in the past found this theory by the non-believers both disturbing and difficult to explain away. I pondered upon it many times, through watching the way my master deals with the disharmony amongst his students, by studying other people and the way they deal with each other especially the way parents deal with their children, then reflecting on these things and the question. Why does God allow violence and cruelty to exist? I found answers for myself. It was hard work but it was worth it.

The observations I made, and my subsequent meditations, were at first clouded by my own horror and shock at the needless violence and aggression which surrounds us in our everyday lives. Then, slowly at first, I began to see times when I myself did or said things that caused others discomfort and distress. I do not regard myself as an aggressive person, yet sometimes, no matter how unintentional, my actions caused others pain or distress. As I continued to study and ponder on this question of why God allowed sin and chaos to exist, my findings at first surprised then astonished me and finally confirmed three things for me. First, my master Chee Soo is the most spiritually developed person I have ever met and I am honoured to be able to study the Taoist Arts with him.

Second, that all people are basically good when you get behind the mask that they present to the world, The mask is an illusion of their real selves which they hide behind to protect themselves for fear that showing their true nature would make them vulnerable. Third, that there is a supreme spirit, God or whatever other name you care to use, and that this supreme spirit is at the same time omnipresent, omniscient and omnipotent. This supreme spirit is not a sectarian God, not belonging to any individual religion but available to all who will recognize that acceptance of this fundamental truth is the first step to harmonizing yourself to the spirit. Then serenity and happiness will follow.

Have you ever watched a baby that has just learnt to crawl? Did you see how excited the baby becomes at its new found freedom? No longer is it confined to its pram, carry-cot or chair with their restraining straps. Watch the baby scurry across the floor so totally absorbed in its adventures that it sees no danger. The delighted parents look on enthralled at their offspring's antics. When the baby crawls towards a chair or table and is in danger of knocking itself the parents either jump up to steer the child clear of the object or shout directions. So the child learns by being guided away from danger by the protective parents. The child also learns through the medium of language. As the parents and others talk, the child learns to recognize the tone of voice that is associated with danger, the understanding of the words comes later. Sooner or later flesh and bone meet some solid object like a chair or table leg. This causes the child pain and if it cries it is comforted by its parents. This is a vital lesson, for the child starts to associate the warning shout or gentle steering away by its parents with the pain that was a result of its collision. Unfortunately this accident will be repeated many times before the child learns that it is folly to crawl at full speed head on to a solid object. The lessons are vital because the child learns to trust its parents' judgement, so later when confronted with potentially more harmful situations after the child has learnt language skills, the child learns to trust the judgement of grown-ups (as all parents know, this state of affairs does not last), and the child has the benefit of these earlier direct experiences on which to base their judgement of the present situation.

The parents can be over-protective and restrict their offspring's freedom by being authoritarian and creating rule after rule that must be obeyed. Or they can allow their child room for personal freedom so that they can develop their self confidence. This will mean allowing them the freedom to make their own mistakes, which they undoubtedly will, in the cause of this great adventure we call life. The love for one's children that this requires is greater by far than that required by the authoritarian parent who seeks to control and unnecessarily restrict.

This is the age old problem of the parents' trying to mould their young into what they would like them to be, or into a career that will make the parents proud of the profession they settle into, regardless of what the child feels. Loving them enough to allow them to make their own mistakes and then being there to help when things go wrong is difficult. Encouraging them to extend themselves while observing their progress with a watchful eye and guiding them when necessary with a gentle hand requires much attention and sacrifice by loving parents on behalf of their off-spring. The child will not always be grateful for this loving care because they - like the fish out of water that thrashes about in the gentle hand that is trying to return it to the stream - will not always understand that the gentle hand you guide them with is motivated by love. Sometimes they will see it as a restrictive force but later when they are older, perhaps with children of their own, they will appreciate that your intentions were pure. So it would seem to me that an important element of love is service to others, without expectations of praise or rewards. Easy to say, easy to write, not so easy to live up to. For understanding it is one thing, putting it into practice is another. If we could all practise being of service to others a little more each day, the world would be a much nicer place for everyone. Most people adopt the attitude that when other people start being nicer to me then I will be nicer to them. Of course most of those other people will be thinking the same thing, so no one will make the first helpful gesture to break the deadlock. Fear of ridicule holds most people back. Conquer that fear and you life will change forever, for the better. In your daily work try to be of more service to others and you will be repaid tenfold - providing that this act of service is performed out of love and NOT with expectations of praise or reward. If you are unfortunate enough to be one of the many people who are unemployed then you can still be of service simply by being pleasant and cheerful to others you come into contact with. Perhaps you could help a neighbour do some job, or take a trip to the shops for a less able relative or neighbour. If you do help your neighbours and relatives in this way you will receive much more in return than you gave, and you will feel all the better for it too.

People who do not believe in the existence of a supreme spirit (God) in my experience tend to be of the opinion that, this life is all you get and therefore you must fight to secure your fair share of everything. Possessions are the most important feature in the lives of these people, fine houses, expensive cars, important and influential friends, exclusive furniture and adornments for their home and a spouse who is admired and respected, or feared by others. And if these lose their value to impress, fail to make others jealous, then they are discarded and replacements are sought. The world's resources are being squandered by those who subscribe to this practice. People's sense of worth is being erased by the constant need to prove themselves successful in a material context. Ambition, greed and aggression in the pursuit of these values reign at the moment. The spiritual values of love, compassion and service are in decline and need to be rekindled if the human race is to develop and prosper.

Why does God allow misery, wrongdoing and violence to exist? It is generally accepted that it is the power of reason that gives us humans supremacy over the other species on earth. This power of reason, bestowed upon us by the supreme spirit, allows us to think things through and make choices. With this gift comes an obligation. When we make a choice and act upon it we must accept responsibility for our actions. When we have children we must accept the responsibility for our action. The birth of a child should not be viewed as an unfortunate side effect of sex. Children born to us are a gift from the almighty, a chance to show how much we have learnt about love and service by doing our best to bring up our children, and passing on our knowledge and understanding to them.

What has all this to do with the question why does God allow pain and suffering to go on in the world? It is my personal belief that God allows these things to happen because he loves us and wants us to learn to love him, not just to say we love him but to show we love him through our actions and service to others. What? I hear you say. God allows pain and suffering to exist because he loves us. You must be mad. Well, perhaps I am but please bear with me while I explain my views before you pass judgement.

God is often referred to as our father which art in heaven. In all religions and philosophies that speak of a Godhead, a divine being or a supreme spirit, whatever name is used is not important, this can be taken for the purpose at hand to mean God. If this offends anyone I would like to point out that whatever name you use, it is only that, a name. It is the sentiment that counts not the name. That out of the way, we can follow on by accepting that God is the creator of life on earth and therefore he is our father, and we are his children. Like a good father should, he watches over his children, but being the supreme spirit, he is wiser and knows more than any human father ever could. He sees everything that we do, all the time, he is omniscient. He lays down rules for behaviour, rules that harmonize with nature. Sensible parents lay down rules for their children to follow. However, Commandments and rules can be broken if you have free will, because you are able to make your own choices. When our children break our house-rules it makes us sad that we have to punish them for their behaviour. Sometimes this is not necessary as the consequences of breaking the rule is punishment enough. When we break one of the natural laws we must suffer as a consequence of our action. God does not sit around heaven all day waiting to catch wrong doers in the act. Their actions create their own punishment. If you cause someone else pain you will find it returns to you, not necessarily immediately or in the same form, but because your action affects someone else. Harmony must be restored, by you being affected also. The choice is ours and when we make a bad choice, either deliberately or through ignorance, we can rely on the Tao (Way) to point out our error so that we may learn to live in accordance with the natural order of things.

God (our father), loves us (his children), and because his love is unlimited, he does not restrict us. He does not deny us free-will by making our every thought and action governed by instinct. Instead he gives us the power of reason so that we may soar to new heights of development in both an earthly and a spiritual way. Whilst we should endeavour to improve our circumstances by making life more comfortable for each other, as well as for ourselves, by improving housing, food supply and things like medical care, we must pay equal attention to our spiritual needs and development. For the things of this world, including the life we are now living, are ephemeral, and just as children grow up into adults and put away childish things and learn to sacrifice their individual wants and wishes on occasions for the good of the family unit, so we must learn to live together with other peoples of the world, especially the indigenous people who live in places like the rain forests of South America and elsewhere. We must not push these people into extinction, merely, because we have the power to do so. They must be allowed to live the kind of life they choose. We are learning quickly that we need the rain forests to maintain the water table and as a possible supply of, as yet, undiscovered life-saving medicine. All the people of the world have a right to live out their lives in a manner of their choosing, providing that it does not interfere with the well-being of others. We must not push people out of their environments and cultures or change them against their will, merely to satisfy our own selfish wants and wishes.

God, our father, head of the family, loves his children. Therefore he gives the power of reason, which gives us his children freedom of choice. And sometimes we, like our own children, cause problems through our own inexperience and lack of understanding. But through this unconditional love given by the father, in the form of freedom of choice and trust, we have the opportunity to learn. The problems of the world, the sin, pain and suffering are not caused by God. They are caused by man's inhumanity to man. Man's greed, the desire to have more for himself. Man's unwillingness to share the fruits of the earth with his neighbour. Animals fight to protect their families and kill to obtain food. Only man fights and kills for pleasure.

Man, because he has been given the power of reason, can, if he wishes, see beyond his own needs, beyond the needs of his family, beyond the needs of his country. We exist together on this earth through the generosity of our maker. We could repay that generosity by sharing what we have with others who have not enough food, clothing or adequate shelter, and by trying to ensure that others everywhere in the world have freedom of choice and do not have to live under an authoritarian regime. Governments of the world must communicate and work together to ensure despots are not allowed to get out of control. The governments of the world must ever be watchful. Like the good gardener who watches over his garden, when it is necessary to weed the garden, he does not shrink from the task. The weeding must be attended to before the weeds take too strong a hold and spread too much, before they start to choke and restrict the growth of the lovely flowers or nourishing foods we are trying to grow. We must pluck them out or cut them back, so our garden is allowed to develop to its full potential. We must not forget or become complacent. History has proved over and over again what the gardener knows from tending his garden, that the climatic conditions that help the garden to astound us with its beauty and provide us with nourishing foods also encourage the weeds to grow. Left unchecked, the weeds can soon take over, choking everything in their path in their greed to gain more and more ground. If this is allowed to happen, the flowers and nourishing foods wither and die. The garden becomes ugly and overgrown. It will then require a sterling gardener, one full of enthusiasm, vision and lack of fear for hard work to bring the garden back to its former glory. Despots, tyrannical rulers and those who would oppress their people, stifling freedom, must not be allowed to develop unchecked.

History tells us through stories like the destruction of Sodom in ancient Palestine, and Noah and his ark, that God will, if he has to, clear his garden and start again. We are his gardeners, his custodians of this planet, our mother earth, which provide us with all we need. If we upset the balance of nature or raise pollution to intolerable levels we will condemn ourselves to extinction. If we become so corrupt we become spiritual morons, spiritually withered and too weak to be saved. God will take a hand and replant his garden. The lessons are all around us if we care to look. We must learn to take time to see and hear the truth. It is not good enough to say, I am too busy making a living to have time for all that, or saying, after I am dead and gone I don't care what happens. Our children will inherit the earth in whatever state we leave it. We ought to endeavour to leave them as bountiful a legacy as possible. If we, through greed, deplete the earth's resources, God will clear the earth and let it stand fallow, let it balance itself before he replants. Our future is in our own hands; we have been given free will, the power of reason, let us use it wisely. God is our father, the earth our mother, and we are their children. To quote from

Ecclesiasticus section seven on how children should conduct themselves in relation to their parents:

With all your heart honour your father, never forget the birth pangs of your mother, remember you owe your birth to them; how can you repay them for what they have done for you?

Love, then, it seems to me, requires service towards the object of your affection, whether it be love of your job, friend, child, wife, husband, the world in which we live, or God. Of course, you should change your job, friends, relationships if they are restrictive to your personal growth. If however you are always unhappy and constantly changing your job, friends or relationships, perhaps instead of looking outwards you should start to look inwards at yourself. It could be that the problem is with yourself. There is a prayer that expresses this point better than I can:

Lord, give me the humility to accept the things I cannot change.

The courage to change the things that ought to be changed.

AND THE WISDOM TO KNOW THE DIFFERENCE.

When we love somebody or something we want to be of service to them or to it. If we love our garden we want to be of service to it, care for it, and it will reward us for our efforts with beautiful flowers and nourishing foods. If we love our work we will work hard and conscientiously with a cheerful disposition. For this we will be rewarded with the satisfaction of a job well done to the best of our ability. We will constantly be looking for ways to be of more service, and the more we give the more we will receive, satisfaction that is, not necessarily more money or promotion. Although if we give willingly of ourselves without any expectation of reward or praise we may find those things come our way too.

God, like the Tao, the natural order of things is unfathomable. We with our limited understanding cannot fathom the working of God or the Tao. God however, can see our actions and fully understands our deeds towards others perfectly well. If our deeds are motivated by greed and lust, HE SEES THIS. If our deeds are motivated by love and respect, HE SEES THIS. There is no hiding place. God is omnipresent and omniscient. Wherever you are he is there with you. Whatever you do, he sees you do it.

There is a saying which I believe comes from the Sufi school of thought: Love is bondage entered into willingly by the free. The use of the word bondage is meant, I believe, to imply subjection to self-restraint, influence and obligation. To love one's job, child, parent or God, one must enter into bondage with the object of that love. Can you love your child and not be a serf serving them? Can you love your child and not be subject to restraining your behaviour and actions on their account on occasions? Can you say you love your child but are not influenced by their behaviour or actions? Is it possible to love your child and not enter into obligations because of them or on their behalf? To love someone or something one has to enter into bondage, without it love cannot be present. Greed, yes. Lust, yes. Ego, yes. Love, NO.

I believe that God wants us to love him but he gives us free choice so we may choose to love or not love him. His love is completely unlimited, therefore he does not place physical or mental restrictions upon us so that we are forced to love him in a limited fashion. He wants to teach us to love truly, purely, but this can only come about if we want it. So he gives us freedom of choice so that we may choose. Taoism says that words are meaningless, it is your actions that are important. Saying you love God and attending church every Sunday is worthless if you are merely paying lip service to God. You must love through your actions. Singing hymns and saying prayers once a week whilst you are behaving in an unchristian way the rest of the week is not good enough. You fool no one but yourself. Remember, God is everywhere and knows everything, and if you think doing the right things while others are watching you, then being unchristian when they are not, will take you to the top of the class you are sadly mistaken.

The analogy between teacher and student is useful in the sense that the teacher (God) understands the student's (our) difficulty, and as the student struggles to gain greater understanding, some of us, like some students at school, do not wish to learn anything, but would, if given the choice skip class and play all day. Some would, and do, study each and every day for long hours, expressing the view that play is a waste of time and not fitting for a superior specimen such as the human race - more often what they really mean is a superior specimen such as them. A balance between play and study will enable each of us to expand and enjoy life to a greater extent while at the same time being able to contribute more. Study is useful so that we may learn from the experience of others who have gone before us and use that knowledge to make us more proficient in our endeavours within our chosen field of work. After all, it would be foolish not to take advantage of the lessons learnt in the past. But that in itself is not enough. We must also learn to implement those lessons, and this means learning to communicate effectively with others. What better way to learn social skills than through the medium of play?

Let us assume that we agree that we must study in order to improve ourselves, whether that improvement is of a temporal or spiritual nature does not matter because the guidance given through scripture shows that the truth is applicable to the external and the internal. When the students attend class and present themselves before the teacher the teacher accepts the student and teaches them the subject. Sometimes the students do not always understand the methods of the teacher, perhaps not readily agreeing that the methods used are the best. The teacher, however, being well versed in the subject, has the understanding to see what the students' needs are to learn the subject. If the student resists the teacher's efforts to teach and does not complete the work set by the teacher, progress will inevitable be slow. To gain the most benefit the students must find a teacher they can work with, then make themselves available to the teacher and put their trust in the teacher. A teacher cannot teach a student who refuses to be taught.

A few years ago I went to college to improve my mathematics, I needed to reach a certain level to be able to take a course in computer studies. One day during the course another student while being assisted by the teacher burst into tears. She complained that she did not understand part of the syllabus, She said she did not want to learn it because she just could not understand it. The teacher calmly explained that it was part of the course and she needed to learn it, she should relax and ask as often as she wished for help and it would be given until she mastered that section. She continued to cry and complain that she did not see why she had to do that part if she did not want to. The tutor asked her why she had enrolled for the course and she said she needed to pass the exam to be able to apply for the job she wanted. He then asked her what mathematics is all about and she said that it was to do with numbers. He then went on to explain that he could teach her anything she wished to learn about numbers and he promised to persevere until she learn the skills required. To pass the exam, he went on to explain, it was required that she learnt and became proficient in this section. 'You have chosen to attend the course to learn mathematics, I will teach you, but you must not ask me why you have to learn this section, because it is part of the course and as such it is a requirement that you learn it. Talk to me about numbers and I can help you, but I cannot help you if you say you do not want to learn them, because I teach people about numbers, that is what I do.' The lady was then advised to take a little walk or go to the canteen for a drink and then return and have another go. Off she went returning sometime later and tried again. The teacher went to her aid promptly when she asked for help. Unfortunately she merely complained that she did not want to learn that part again. He calmly and reassuringly explained that he could only help her if they talked in terms of numbers and he would persevere until she understood. She eventually got up and left the room and I learnt later she left the course. Many people have a fear of mathematics, but it can, like any fear, be overcome with the help of a conscientious and sincere teacher. This lady found such a teacher. Unfortunately she would not allow him to teach her. Finally, she left. The teacher did not desert her; she left the teacher. God is a conscientious and sincere teacher, and because his love is unlimited and his generosity is boundless he gave us free will that we may choose our own path. When we leave our predestined path and our life turns into chaos, he waits patiently for us to return.

I hope I do not offend anyone by pointing out that if you reverse the letters in God you get the word dog. A dog is a wonderful friend and companion. Forget to feed it, ignore it when you are too busy and go out and leave it on its own for hours. Does it complain when you return? No, instead it jumps up at you and licks your hands and face and showers you with affection. Under the same conditions do you know any human being that would do the same? God's love is like that, it is truly unlimited, and if you have strayed from the path, do not fear retribution if you return to him because he will shower you with affection and show you how pleased he is that you have returned again to your rightful home.

Love is bondage entered into willingly by the free. I could never remember this phrase. Every time I wanted to recall it I would get it all mixed up. Then the lovely lady I mentioned earlier came into my life and one day while we were talking I quoted it for the first time without any hesitation or error. This lady is my special lady, and like the Yin and Yang she is my opposing yet complementary factor. Bonded together, we unite and become a whole unit. Complementing each other and working together, I know we will make a greater contribution than we ever could as individuals. I have a love for the Taoist Arts taught to me by Master Chee Soo that is a very unique love, because teaching these arts to others so they can improve their health and spiritual well-being is the way I give service to God. I believe, because of my service to others in the face of adversity and pressure to conform to what is considered a normal lifestyle, I have been sent this lovely lady with whom to share my life. We are so utterly compatible it constantly shocks me. This does not mean we do not have disagreements, because we do. But we work them out because we both know we are right for each other. Neither of us could explain this through the use of logic. We just know. I have free will and I have chosen to enter into bondage with this woman freely and my life has been enriched beyond my wildest dreams. When I recognized that I was destined to learn and teach the Taoist arts, and willingly subjected myself to this, my life was enriched. Teaching the Taoist arts with this wonderful lady by my side I enjoy a serenity and happiness greater than any I have ever known. I thank the Lord daily for these gifts and I try to give others some of the benefits I have received from the practise of the Taoist arts. This is my service to God and humanity. During these troubled times with all the unemployment and lack of direction in peoples lives, it may be a humble task but I am eternally grateful for it because it allows me to be useful to society and gives my life purpose and meaning.

My Master

My teacher Master Chee Soo inherited the Lee family style of T'ai Chi, the self defence arts of Feng Shou and Ch'i Shu, and the health arts from his master Chan Kam Lee, who having no family of his own adopted Chee Soo as his nephew. Born in 1919, Chee Soo started his training with Chan Kam Lee in the summer of 1934. After the death of Chan Lee, Master Chee Soo became president of the Cultural Arts Association which in recent years has been renamed The International Taoist Arts Society. As well as having many clubs throughout the British Isles, the International Taoist Society now has clubs that are well established in France, Germany, Holland and Australia.

Master Chee Soo has devoted his life to the practice and teaching of the Taoist Arts, and anyone who has ever been to one of his classes will have seen for themselves the enthusiasm and love he has for these Chinese arts. People who have trained with him in the self defence arts of Feng Shou and Ch'i Shu often see him as an extremely skillful and powerful fighter. People who have trained with him in the art of T'ai Chi and K'ai Men see him as an amazingly sensitive man who has great understanding and control over the natural energies that are harnessed or are constantly passing through the body. His phenomenal control over his own body and mind which at times is, simply superhuman. The many thousands of people who have been helped by him, free of charge, though his knowledge of the health arts see him as a gentle, compassionate and generous man. He is all these things and more. He is amazingly healthy and strong, internally as well as externally. He has great awareness of his own body and the energies that it utilizes. At 75 years old, he trains with, and is physically and mentally superior to, men and woman in their twenties and thirties. But most important of all, whether it is through the auspices of Self-defence, T'ai Chi, K'ai Men or the health arts, his continual benevolence is an example to all who have been fortunate enough to meet and train under him. He teaches people, through the medium of Kung Fu, to learn to control the physical expression of their emotions. Fear, aggression, weaknesses and strengths must all be examined and brought under control. First however you must recognize these things in yourself. You cannot control something that you deny exists. We all experience fear, aggression, pain and pleasure. If you deny these things exist in you, then you are foolish and you allow them to dictate your behaviour. If however, you actively seek them out, examine them, then you will be able to bring them under your control. Through T'ai Chi, K'ai Men and the Health arts, Master Chee Soo shows those who are prepared to listen how they can improve their health, beyond what they hitherto thought possible. He does not force the Taoist Long Life diet (Chang Ming) upon people. He states the benefits and supplies sheets with the dietary recommendations. He is himself the best advertisement for the Chang Ming diet. He practises what he preaches, unlike many western physicians.

The Lee family crest, which was passed on to Chee Soo By Chan Kam Lee, is a seahorse. The International Taoists Societies' badge is a circular emblem showing the Yin and Yang sign with a seahorse wearing a coolie's hat in the centre. The circle shows that we are one family. The Yin and Yang symbol shows the two opposing yet complementary factors within any family and everything within the universe. The seahorse in the centre represents the head of the family and is a symbol of the principles the head of the family endeavours to uphold. There are twenty species of seahorse, half of which live in the Indo-Australian region. The others live off the Atlantic coasts of Europe, Africa, North America and the Pacific coast of America. When the seahorse mates, the male pairs off with a female and she inserts her long ovipositor into the male's pouch, which is situated on his belly, there she lays her eggs, as many as two hundred. While this takes place, the mouth of the male pouch is large, but when the female has finished laying her eggs his pouch closes to a minute pore, and stays this way during the gestation period of 4 - 5 weeks. When the young have hatched and are ready to be born, the pouch opens. The male seahorse bends and then straightens its body in convulsive jerks until finally a baby seahorse shoots out through the mouth of the pouch. They are about $1/2$ inch long at birth and perfect miniature replicas of their parents. The male rests after each birth and shows signs of extreme exhaustion when all the babies are born. Kept in aquariums, the males often die after giving birth. In their natural environment however, this does not occur, and the male seahorse is soon looking round for a female to fill his pouch with eggs again.

To me, my Master is the perfect embodiment of these principles. He is the head of our family and he nurtures his offspring (his students) with great care. His pouch (training hall) is always open to newcomers. Once they have entered he will nurture (train) them with great care and attention. And when they are grown physically, mentally and spiritually he will open his pouch that they may be born and go forth and live and multiply (having become teachers themselves they may now repay the debt and teach others). He exists for his family and for his work, which is teaching the Taoists Arts. The coolie's hat worn by the seahorse is a symbol of humility. Many times I have watched my Master walk round the training hall picking up bits of paper, cotton thread and other litter while some instructor has been designated to conduct the warm up exercises. In full view of his students, he shows he is prepared to do the most menial task himself. I once saw him use a vacuum cleaner that had been left in the training hall. He turned it on, and off he went round the hall cleaning the place up. Everyone, including myself, was amused to see the Master vacuuming the place. I was taking the warming up exercise session and enjoyed the fun too when he stuck the vacuum on my training trousers in an unfortunate place. However, I survived the experience intact. I have met no other Master whose ego and self importance would not forbid him from performing such a menial task as cleaning up the training hall himself. Yes, Master Chee Soo, you wear the coolie's hat, and you wear it with dignity and pride. I feel deeply honoured to have you as my spiritual teacher. Those of us who are fortunate enough to be able to train under him are obliged to do our best to grow physically, mentally and spiritually so that we may carry on this work as others have before us, so that others may have the opportunity to study the Taoist Arts. Their value is as relevant today as it was in ancient times. The truth will always be the truth. The way of the Tao will remain, regardless of man's interference. Ecclesiasties 1:4 'A generation goes, a generation comes, yet the earth stands firm for ever'. It has been my honour and privilege to be a student of Master Chee Soo for the past twenty years. During that time he has beaten me physically, confused and tortured me mentally, and emotionally battered me to pieces. There was no malice in his treatment of me, he was not showing his superiority to bolster his ego, although I am sure to those looking on it must at times have seemed that way. He did it for me, to train me. We learn by suffering discomfort and pain whether that discomfort and pain be physical, mental or emotional. If you doubt the validity of that, then consider the child that has just learnt to crawl. Eager to experience its new found freedom, it crawls excitedly around, and sooner or later bumps into solid objects and hurts itself, and no amount of advice given by the parents or others really influences the child. Its the direct experience that counts, that's what does it. And that is the essence of the Taoist arts; it is the doing that counts, the direct experience. Remember when you were at school and you did not complete your homework on time, remember the mental anguish as you waited to tell the teacher. Remember squirming as you waited to be punished by your parents for some misdemeanour. The mental discomfort certainly made you think twice before repeating the offence, didn't it? So I have suffered in the cause of my training, and had I known at the outset the extent of that suffering I doubt I would have continued. However, my Master being the benevolent and compassionate man that he is, kept this fact from me. Many times I wondered why I continued spending my weekends turning myself into a physical and mental wreck while others went off seeking pleasure and indulging themselves. Well, now in my fifties, I have the physical abilities and health many in their twenties envy and I have an optimism and zest for life that seems to have disappeared from the lives of most of my contemporaries. So I sincerely mean this when I say, "Thank you for the training, Master."

Chan Kam Lee made a wise decision when he left the Arts to Chee Soo. Under his guidance the Taoist Arts have flowered and grown in this and other countries, bringing health, happiness and purpose to the lives of many thousands of people. Chee Soo joins the long list of dedicated Masters who have given of themselves unselfishly for the benefit of others. Someone once said, 'There is no nobler an act a man can do than lay down his life for another'. That is the lot of a Master,. He dedicates his life in the service of others. I owe this man a debt I cannot hope to repay, but then again, he never asked me to repay anything, he just gave, asking nothing in return. He does not suffer from false pride. During the last twenty years that I have known him he has moved four times, each time to a completely new area of the country. Once there he has set about introducing the Taoist arts and training instructors. Of course, the faithful few have always had to follow him. Sometimes the journey to training weekends became shorter, sometimes longer, and during that time I have seen many drop out, unable or unwilling to make the changes necessary in their personal lives. I have been fortunate in being able to alter my circumstances so that I have always been able to continue my training. But it has not always been easy, and my dedication has caused me much suffering. I try to follow the example of my Master as best I can. Ho moves to an area, introduces the Taoist arts, trains instructors and then moves on to another area. In other words he does his work and when the work is done he moves on and starts again. Moving to wherever he is needed, he asks for no praise or reward, he builds up an area then leaves it to others to carry on the work he started. He claims no possessions. Whatever the personal discomfort, he seeks only to serve and do the work that the Tao has allotted him. Often he has been criticized by those he leaves behind. They feel that he came and introduced them to the Taoists arts, and then when he moves on they feel he has taken something away from them. Of course, this is not true. All he ever did was give to them, and at first they are exceedingly grateful for the many gifts he bestowed upon them. But then later, when they have to make some personal sacrifice - in other words make some effort - like travelling a longer distance which takes up more of their time and money, they complain it is not fair, that they are being cheated. Why should he take himself off and teach others, when they are still there willing to learn? Well, the price (effort) goes up, just like inflation. Sometimes it is stable, as, for example, when he once moved and, for me, the distance and cost to travel to the training weekends were the same. Once, the distance, became less as he moved closer to where I lived, and this was like the occasion when inflation goes down, and we all know that this is a very rare occasion indeed. Just as in everyday life, if you want to obtain some goods or service you have to pay the asking price. And inflation can push up the price, as we all know only too well. If we really want the goods we must pay the asking price. Rare and specialist goods require a little more effort to obtain and are more expensive. They are not usually in a shop at the bottom of the street.

Those who choose not to make the extra effort and bear the extra expense required to continue their development by following and training under the Master, tend to be bitter and complain that they were not given enough. They seem to think that he is their personal possession and should be available to them any and every time they require him, without any effort on their part. He, however, has learnt to control his emotions and does not become bitter at their unjustified comments, but continues to serve wherever he can be of most use, doing what he does best, teaching the Taoist Arts. Just like the seahorse, he takes the seeds and gives them nourishment and then when they are ready to enter the world and begin their own adventure in life he moves on and looks for another batch to father in the unique way that only the seahorse is capable of doing. Those previous children, who are grown and now parents themselves, are with their father's permission free to visit him with their families and they will gain further knowledge from their father who has now a wisdom gained from the passing years. And so it is that I, now a teacher myself, continue to travel many miles to train with my Master whenever I can, encouraging my own students to join me because I know that children learn much from their grandfather's wisdom. And I know that parents can learn from their own children too, and that is what I love to do, practise and learn, passing on what I have learnt to others who are seekers of an understanding of the Tao.

To quote from the Tao Te Ching, 'The Tao That Can Be Spoken Of Is Not The Eternal Tao'. The way of nature cannot be understood by reading books or talking (although if these mediums lead you to a Master then they have done their task), but by observing and practising the Taoist arts under the guidance of a Master who himself understands the Tao of his own life and through this has learnt to understand the way (Tao). The true Tao cannot be spoken of, but it can be understood if you are dedicated enough. I have been fortunate indeed to be chosen as a student of this unique Master. I will do my best to follow the principles taught to me, and endeavour to help others by teaching the benefits of the Taoist arts.

Reincarnation

Reincarnation, the rebirth of a soul in a new body, is for most people an interesting subject. Opinions are divided into two camps. There are those who believe that when you die, that is the end. These people say that when you die, you come to a full stop. You only get one life, so you had better make the most of it. People in the other camp hold the view that when the physical body wears out and we die, our soul/spirit returns to either Heaven or the domain of the supreme spirit, depending on your beliefs. I myself follow this view. For me it is not merely a hypothesis, for me it is the truth, with example upon example present in nature. I also believe that when we die the soul/spirit enters Heaven/the spiritual domain and rests and reflects on the good achieved in the past life, and with the guidance of wiser souls/spirits decides on the conditions that will be most beneficial for the next life. The conditions of the next life will, if dealt with correctly, enhance the soul's/spirit's development. This development continues until the illusion of the self is completely annihilated. Then, when the soul/spirit is purified, stripped of the ego, it returns to unite with God/The supreme spirit from whence we came in the beginning. The journey is long and arduous until we see the natural way of things and learn to work within this framework. By ceasing to resist the natural order of things we begin to slowly see the truth and earn for ourselves a freedom that is beyond the comprehension of those chained to their well paid jobs. Often, these well paid jobs give them little satisfaction other than earning money to buy more and more illusions of happiness and achievement.

On what do I base my belief in reincarnation? Many, many things to me, confirm the theory of reincarnation. Matter, as science has proved, cannot be destroyed, it can only be changed. An example of this is water. If the temperature is lowered enough the water turns to ice. It has not been destroyed but it has been changed because the conditions surrounding it have altered. Again using the example of water, if the temperature is raised enough the water becomes steam. It has not been destroyed but its state has been changed.

Flowers bloom and our spirits are uplifted by their beauty. Then they die off but they are not destroyed. Either the bulbs lie sleeping, resting in the soil gaining replenishment, or, before they die, shed their seeds which bury themselves in the soil and are nurtured and nourished by mother earth until such times as the conditions are right for them to bloom again. If you examine flowers closely you will see that within their respective groups daffodils, tulips or whatever they appear to be all the same but upon closer inspection you will see that each one is unique, no two are exactly alike. Just like human beings, there are northerners, southerners, black people, white people. Yet within these groups no two are exactly alike; each person, like each individual flower, is unique.

Trees and bushes remain visible above ground all year round while their roots remain hidden under ground where they gain nourishment and provide stability for the trunk and branches. During the season the trees and bushes give forth their flowers, fruits and nuts and we are able to harvest their beauty with our eyes and collect their fruits and nuts along with the rest of the animal kingdom to nourish and sustain our bodies so that we may live on. When we eat the food provided by the plant world we do not destroy it, we change it. Our bodies break down the food and distribute it through the systems of the body to build tissue to replace that which is worn out and also to provide the necessary ingredients to sustain life. What is left over is discarded by the body. This waste matter becomes food and nourishment for other insects and plants. So the chain continues with everything depending on everything else for survival. And during this process matter is changed many times from one state to another, but it is not destroyed, it continues in another form.

Well cared for, the plants and trees provide better quality food, a lesson in itself, for to receive care and attention we must first give care and attention. To receive love we must first give love. There is no doubt that trees and plants well looked after provide the best harvest. If we could only see the lessons clearly. If we could have the sense to follow nature, the natural way, and show our love for our fellow humans by our acts of service, the love we gave and received in return would abolish much of the hardship, poverty and suffering present in the world today. But it does require actions, words are not enough. Waiting for somebody else to do it will not solve the problem either. We can all do something, no matter how humble that something is. If we all managed to do one small act on a regular basis in the service of humanity, that small act multiplied by the millions of people who are able to make the gesture, would add up to a bigger contribution than any one person or government could make.

Most of us are active during the daylight hours and sleep during the darkness of night. While we rest, our body is still active, repairing the damage done by the ravages of the day on our tired muscles and frayed nerves. So are we alive or dead when we sleep? I suppose it depends on your definition of alive. Or are there different states of being alive or dead? Well I suppose you could say that to be alive is to be actively doing something, be that something a physical action or some mental activity. Does this then mean that when we sleep we are really dead? Or are we like the bulbs, merely resting, conforming to a natural cycle that creates a balance between activity and rest resulting in a healthy body? During sleep the body takes the nourishment consumed through the day and rejuvenates the body. The cells of the body, imbued with fresh vitality, are now ready to deal with the stresses and strains of the coming day. In the deep recesses of the mind the brain completes an analysis of the days events, sifting through the information received and the experiences gained. From this, messages are passed to the spirit, and the spirit passes back advice on the advisable procedure to follow in the future. We call these hunches. I am sure that most of you will have been told at some time or other by a parent or peer when faced with a difficult decision 'to sleep on it' and then having taken that advice, awoke knowing the answer to your problem the following morning. These hunches, if acted upon on a regular basis, become more prolific. If, however, you do not act on your hunches but continually go against them - humans beings are given free will and can chose to ignore the advice given through the spirit - the hunches, the flashes of intuition, will appear to you less and less frequently and your life will become more and more fraught. The ensuing turmoil is merely a lesson to tell you that you are going about things the wrong way, and it will continue until you learn to listen to the little voice within, your guiding spirit.

Too much activity and too little sleep will set your nerves on edge and the body and brain will be unable to function at their best, eventually running the body down to such an extent that illness will follow. Too much sleep and too little activity will make the body and mind dull and lethargic, leading to apathy and other more serious forms of illness. Balance, again, is the key word, and we must all find our own balance, for we are all unique, no two are exactly the same. Eight hours sleep may be too much for one person and yet not enough for another. Each must find their own balance which may vary according to the conditions surrounding that person at the time.

So it would seem that being awake and being asleep are only

different states of consciousness. When we are awake we are not resting - we are aware of all that goes on within and around us,. Or are we? When we are asleep we rest and all physical and mental activity ceases. Or does it?

Let's look at these two questions separately. First, when we are awake we are fully alert and aware of all that happens around us and of course we are obviously conscious of our own actions, in other words we known what we are doing. Or do we? During my training in the Taoist arts I have come to realize that many things that I thought were natural, that everybody did automatically and therefore required no conscious thought, do in fact require great mental control and awareness to be performed efficiently. Simple daily acts such as walking and breathing require great personal awareness. Anybody who has walked into a lamppost or stubbed their toe on a doorstep, or nearly had an accident riding their bicycle or driving their car will readily be able to see that being conscious of and being present in NOW, moment to moment, being consciously aware of our actions is extremely difficult. The Taoist theory of 'non action' appertains to this but is often misunderstood. It does not mean that you should sit under a tree all day contemplating the meaning of life. 'Non action' is not an excuse to be lazy. No! what 'non action' means is that instead of interfering with things, insisting that your way is better and trying to bully everyone into doing things your way, the way of non action is to join in, not exclude yourself from life, see what skills you have, see where those skills would be useful, and then make them available to those in need. In this way you do not oppose the natural flow of things but enhance it. Of course, to do this you must be able to see things as they are, not as you think they should be. Be able to exercise humility in the service of others without expectations of reward or praise. To be present in the moment, to see what is required of you and give it willingly and consciously without any expectations for the future and without any thoughts of the past. Expectations lead to disappointments. If you are performing a task merely for expectation of reward, the reward is never great enough and you will become unhappy and bitter. While you are performing the task your mind will be not on the task at hand, but ahead, thinking of what you will do with the reward you expect or how everyone else will be jealous of the praise you will receive. Not where it should be, in the present, giving your full attention to the task at hand. You cannot perform the task to your fullest capabilities and therefore the reward will match this.

Whatever the financial gain, it will never be enough. If, however, you can genuinely perform some task, merely out of the joy of doing it well, and in the service of others without any expectation, your reward will always exceed your expectations and you will feel such gratitude that you will endeavour to be of greater service. Your life will be happy and you will feel fulfilled. And, because you give your full attention to each task that you do, you are living life to the full, in the present. You will develop greater skills and become of greater and greater service and will therefore earn for yourself greater and greater rewards. So, while we are awake we can endeavour to be fully awake in the present or only partially awake by not being steeped in the present but partly in the future, which has not yet been born. Taoist philosophy teaches that our own personal reality is right here, now. The meaning of life is living it, now. Yesterday has gone, never to return. The future has not yet been born. Here, right now, is real. Living for the present, moment to moment, is to live life to the full. Action in 'non action' by doing nothing you accomplish everything.

When we sleep do we die a little death until we awake in the morning, conscious once more of life and our surroundings? When we go to sleep our perception certainly changes. We close our eyes to the outside world and stop taking in the vast amounts of information that during our waking hours constantly bombard our senses. We lay our body down, making ourselves comfortable, so that our physical body may rest. This lack of physical activity, along with the fact that the body does not ingest food during sleep, allows the body to repair worn out tissues and the internal organs can rest themselves. All the functions of the body must rest and recuperate to regain the energy expended during the period when they were active. But the major organs of the body do not stop altogether but merely take it in turns to rest, while others perform their tasks of repairing and revitalizing the body.

Medical science has shown that the brain's activity changes during sleep from light to deep sleep. Without delving too deeply into this, science is beginning to learn, through Quantum Physics and the Chaos Theory with its now famous butterfly effect, that everything in the cosmos depends on and is effected by everything else. Medical science is slowly starting to realize what the alternative medical practitioners have known for a long time, that all the functions of the body depend on each other and distribute nutrients and energies to and from one another. So that if one should cease to function correctly then others will suffer a loss also. It is also known, albeit not yet greatly recognized, that all illness stems from the mind before it becomes a physical manifestation in the body, and that going further back' illness is born of disharmony between the spirit and body. The reason for the great variety of illnesses in existence today is the movement of man further and further away from spiritual values in the pursuit of material gain. It is my belief that the seeds of all illness are ever present in the world and that under certain conditions they prosper. Just as the weeds prosper if we neglect the garden, taking it over and choking everything in their greed for a larger portion of ground and sunlight. We have for too long neglected our communal garden 'THE EARTH AND ITS INHABITANTS'. We do so at our peril because, as science is showing us through the medium of Chaos

Theory and Quantum Physics, and as nature has always shown us through example after example, as when we turned fertile land into dust-bowls and deserts, as when over-fishing the sea has caused the near extinction of certain species. All because of our greed to extract more and more for our personal prosperity. Our short term gain is our long term destruction. Everything depends on everything else for its healthy existence. We cannot pollute the rivers and kill the fish, spray poisons on our crops to kill insects, pollute the air with our factories and motor vehicles, spill oil and dump waste in the sea, and then expect the air we breathe, the food we eat and the water we drink to be healthy. It is my belief that the diseases that are rampant in our society today are a product of our spiritual disharmony. The lack of love and compassion for our follow mankind and nature produces heart disease. Greed, the striving for more and more material possessions and pleasures leads to cancer. The unnatural sexual practices designed to fulfil the desire for greater and greater sexual pleasure encourage venereal diseases, Aids and child abuse.

How do we eradicate these diseases? Not by oppression or by making more and more laws that restrict man's freedom! But by cultivating the spiritual values, the lack of which is the root cause of their existence. I believe that if we learn to love and care for our mother earth, and all the inhabitants of our planet, this spiritual value will erase heart disease. I believe that if we stop greedily trying to amass more and more possessions, stop collecting more and more wealth at the expense of others, sharing instead what we have with those less fortunate than us, then the disease of cancer, which is an abnormal and uncontrollable division of body cells in excess of the normal production required to replace worn out cells, will disappear. If a man and woman love and cherish each other, if their relationship is built on honesty and trust, they will be able to enjoy a fulfilling partnership in all their activities, including lovemaking, without the use of mechanical aids or pornographic material. They will then have no need to indulge in unnatural sexual practices. Male and female are the two opposing yet complementary factors necessary for the continuation of any species. If man and woman demand satisfaction from each other, craving more and more sexual experiences, this will inevitably lead to degenerative behaviour and conflict within the relationship. If, however, the two partners constantly show their love for each other, assisting each other, if their actions are complementary rather than conflicting, they must inevitably fulfil and enhance each others lives. Sex without love is a poor substitute for the real thing. When a man and woman who are truly in love, embrace each other, they enter a state of bliss that no mechanical aid or pornographic film or experience-enhancing drug can compare with. For when a man and woman join together in love, losing their individuality and coupling their life energies and spirits together, they unite and become one and their spirits soar to the heavens.

So I believe that as day turns to night and then returns to day again, not the same day, but another new exciting adventurous day, as the trees and bushes loose their leaves and fruits, then regain new leaves and fruits the next season, as the flower blooms and then the beautiful petals fade away but the bulbs or seeds bury themselves in mother earth and await the new season's arrival when they can again flower and show the beauty and unlimited diversity of the Tao/God, as water from the sea evaporates into the atmosphere, forms clouds and when the conditions are right falls to earth as rain, soaks into the earth and nourishes all life and then flows via the streams and rivers back to the sea again whence the process repeats itself, so man's physical body fades away and his spirit returns to the spirit world to rest and recuperate, there to wait for suitable conditions to occur so that he may again take human form, and have the chance to further develop his spirit.

I also believe that if we greedily rob, violate and pollute the land, sea and air, continue with our acts of cruelty and exploitation towards the animal kingdom and our fellow men, we will be the cause of our own annihilation. Then we would have to wait for the earth to repair itself, before it became habitable again, delaying our own spiritual development. As it says in Ecclesiastes 1:4 Man comes and goes but the earth abides. Our resistance to the natural flow of things (The Tao) is the cause of our own suffering. If on the other hand we learn to care for our planet, care for the animal kingdom, care for our fellow man, we can enjoy nourishing food to eat, clean pleasant-tasting water to drink, fresh, clean air to breathe. Our bodies will become healthy and strong, naturally, and our minds will become calm and free of fear, and we will eradicate disease once and for all.

Some of you may be thinking, boy! this guy's a dreamer. Well, dreams can come true you know. But you do have to have faith and work towards that dream to turn it into a reality. Someone once dreamt they could develop a system that would enable people to communicate over long distances. Because that man had faith and worked at turning his dream into reality, today we have the telephone. Someone once dreamt of the streets free of the stench of waste and rubbish which was not only unpleasant but hazardous to health. Sewerage systems were constructed and health was improved, the streets became cleaner and more pleasant places to be. No longer did people need to walk about, holding a scented handkerchief to their noses. There are many other examples of dreams which became reality, space flight, trains, ocean-going ships, advances in medicine. Some of them good, some not so good. Man has free choice, we have the power to keep the good and reject the bad.

How do we bring these changes about? By actions. If you want to accomplish anything of value or develop some skill it always requires some effort on your part. The greater the skill the more effort required to acquire it. We learn this in many ways. As children, we learn that to acquire the skills necessary to ride a bicycle, we must put in quite a lot of effort and suffer many disappointments before we are successful. The same applies to drawing, writing, swimming and other skills. So if we want to make the world a better place then we must make some effort, and we must be prepared to suffer some disappointments along the way. It is no good blaming everyone else for polluting the environment. We must ensure that we do not allow it in our children, we must teach our children to respect the environment and look after it, teach them to care for wildlife, not fear it, considering wildlife competition for food and land, and therefore an enemy. We must curb our greed and learn to share the planets' bounty with all its inhabitants. We can refuse to buy products from companies that damage the environment or spoil the land or sea. It has been proved that these companies soon change their policies when they start to lose business. We do not have to march about shouting and making a nuisance of ourselves trying to get things changed. We have the ability to do it, if we have the will. If we do not buy products from companies that damage the environment, they must change their ways or go out of business. So the people in a democracy do have the capacity to change things. We must see that we use that authority wisely for the good of everyone, and we should make our elected representatives aware that we expect them to carry out our wishes, and if necessary remind them that they are in office as our elected representatives. Democracy is a system of government by the whole population. Let us withhold our purchases for the products of companies that damage the environment and wildlife. If there are no alternative products available, then let us do without, rather than encourage the damage. And let us vote for the parties that include in their policies the protection of the environment and our wildlife.

We all dream of a brave new world for our children to grow up in.

Well then, let us turn that dream into a reality by working towards it, now, not, put it off until tomorrow or leave it to someone else. We can all do something to change our environment for the better. We can start by realizing what a beautiful place the world is and how fortunate we are to be here. This gift of life given to us is a precious thing, not to be squandered seeking pleasure upon pleasure for the body. Too much of a good thing is bad for you. We should see that this life is a preparation for the next and we should therefore be cultivating spiritual values. By doing this we will love and care for all of God's creation. Man needs to learn to love and appreciate the working of the supreme spirit once again. Then, instead of raping the land and sea, stripping it until it is barren, he will care for and appreciate the Lord's creation. Then, instead of man's self imposed trammel he will be able to soar to new heights of freedom. He will become like the butterfly which breaks out of its restrictive cocoon to find a brave, exciting new world, where he can move with a freedom hitherto undreamt of. A world where there are no limitations, and mans spirit can soar freely and develop unhampered, free at last from constraint. But it will not happen without action, for it is action that turns dreams into reality.

T'ai Chi and the Future

What has an ancient art like Tai Chi to offer in these modern times? Through the practice of Tai chi one becomes in touch with one's body, in tune with one's own mind and also learns to cultivate, harness and utilize the energies inherent in all living things. Firstly, you can learn to know yourself. And, by coming to understand yourself, constantly being aware of all that you do, the thoughts that you have and the emotions that these thoughts breed in you, you can learn to take control of yourself. Then, as you learn to cultivate these changes within you, you will find yourself making a greater contribution to society. You may not notice these changes taking place within, as you will be too busy watching, too busy being aware of how you conduct yourself in your daily life, in your relationship with others. Others will notice the difference in you. And so you will teach by example, not by force. You will not tell anyone how they should conduct themselves, you will not suffer in the battles fought daily by others who try to make their contemporaries follow rules and regulations born out of their own power-seeking minds. By conducting yourself as best you can within the restrictions of everyday life, you will have a freedom only dreamt of by others who seek to impose their will on each other, and who must therefore do battle every day of their lives.

We can only change the negative things in life into positive things by making a change within ourselves. If we try to change others by coercion or by bullying them into following rules made by us, surely this can only create constant conflict. If, however, we can by watching ourselves in our relationship with other people, make a change for the better within ourselves, does this not improve things for ourselves, and others we come into contact with, without creating disharmony?

There are many similarities between modern technology and human life. The computer, man's new toy, needs input, which is like the information we gather from our actions, our relationship with others and our environment. This is our human experience. A computer reacts to the information it is given, which is like the human response to an experience. The computer then puts a label or name on the result and records it in its memory bank, just as human memory is a collection of past experiences. The difference is that human beings are a part of nature and have the ability to raise themselves above pure logical thought. Relying on logical thought is fear of life. Logic has its place, but to live by logic alone is to restrict freedom and produce robotic response.

People like to be told what to do because they fear having to think for themselves. If they have a set of rules to live by they feel protected. They may be protected, but they are also prisoners in a jail which they built themselves, walked into, locking the door behind them, and then threw away the key. The key of life is a precious gift and should not be discarded. Instead we should endeavour to overcome our fears so we may live in freedom. We should not constantly repeat the mistakes of the past because we are afraid to be creative, afraid to take a different approach. The gift of life allows us to be in a constant state of learning. We can only learn if we constantly face the new, the unknown. To live in the known, to be fearful of the new, is to stagnate, to be without life. The problems of the world cannot be solved by repeating the mistakes of the past. A new approach is needed. To have an idea of what the future should be is to try to mould the future into what we want it to be, which inevitably breeds conflict. We must live in the present, spontaneously reacting to our relationship with others and our environment. This is creative living, doing what we can to help others by doing what we like best. Our contribution to society can only be maximized if we are following a vocation that we enjoy, doing something that we love to do, regardless of the material return. This, then, I believe should be our aim, to find out what we like doing best and do it. Then and only then will we by happy. And a happy person is not destructive. Watch your children and you will see that when they are doing something they love to do, something that is creative, they are happy, and when they are happy they are not disruptive.

We must be careful not to fill our children with fear, fear to try something new. Fear is our enemy and we should try to teach our children along with ourselves that making mistakes is a part of life that no-one can avoid. Restricting your activities for fear of making mistakes does nothing to enhance your self development or self esteem. We are all children of the Tao and as such are unique individuals, all capable of contributing to the service of mankind in some way, and we can all continue to learn so that that contribution can be increased. We should not fear mistakes or problems resulting from our actions. We learn by making mistakes. Natural catastrophes such as Earthquakes bring chaos, but they also bring the opportunity to build again. Using the knowledge gained from past experience we can build new, stronger and better, whether we are rebuilding a house or city, or rebuilding a personal relationship or relations between nations. The opportunities are always there but we must move forwards and not hold back for fear of making mistakes. To stand still is to stagnate, to move forwards with the tide of life is to be forever creative. Living in the present is the only possibility for true happiness. I believe that happiness can only come, not from pleasing the senses, but from our relationship with, and our unselfish acts in the service of, others. T'ai Chi has given me so many gifts, gifts of friendships, gifts of knowledge and perhaps the most important gift of all, the gift of good health. I now feel duty bound to try to present these benefits to others. Through teaching T'ai Chi to others I improve my relationship with others and I am also of service to those who wish to learn. I am a lucky man indeed because I have found my path, I have found what I like to do. And in doing it I make a contribution to the good health of others, and I am able to offer T'ai Chi as a tool to others with which they can put themselves in touch with their bodies and minds, so that they to can have the opportunity of finding their own path within themselves. The practice of T'ai Chi teaches the student to live in the present, moment to moment being totally aware of their own actions, thoughts and emotions. They learn to see themselves and others as they really are, now, not as they were yesterday, not as they intend to be tomorrow but just as they are, right now. As they become more aware of themselves and others they are able to relate more effectively with others and also with their own children, teaching them by example.

Tree-growth, unchecked, produces seeds and fruit that become smaller and of poorer quality as the tree grows bigger, and more out of control. A wise and experienced gardener will prune the tree correctly and improve the quality of its fruit; he seeks constantly to improve his work which improves the quality of the fruit and thereby benefits mankind, this is his service to others.

A man concerned with his own material growth, only to make himself richer and more powerful, with no thought of doing good for others, has little benefit to offer mankind. Such a person becomes greedy, wishing to acquire more and more material wealth or power, and keep it for himself. The lessons he teaches do not produce harmony between men. If, however, a man has humility, he can still be materially rich but like the tree his humility acts as self-pruning and his fruit, the lessons he teaches by his actions, will be good quality lessons and his contribution to mankind will be greater.

Two of the main benefits of T'ai Chi are the relaxation it produces in the body and the meditative effect it has on the mind. However, without proper understanding, sometimes the cure can produce more problems. A tense body stems from a tense mind and by trying to learn T'ai Chi many students often try to acquire peace and tranquillity, therefore it eludes them. For the very effort which is used to acquire the relaxed and meditative state produces conflict between the mind and body, and therefore produces tension. So, instead of trying to acquiring things, we must learn to throw the things away that hinder our progress, competitiveness, tension, preconceived ideas of what we will or should attain or experience from T'ai Chi, and just feel what happens and be aware of how we are.

We people of the world must learn to work with nature and not oppose it in our greed to increase our material wealth and physical comfort at the expense of others or of the environment. We live in a crazy world where strange things happen, like the forcing of water production so there is enough for industry as well as human consumption. The process of producing water in large enough quantities requires the use of many chemicals to make it fit for drinking. So we produce large quantities of water to sustain industries that produce an abundance of goods, and in the process of their production many chemicals are produced, many of which find their way into the rivers and lakes via air or land, and more chemicals are used again to purify the water as best we can. These goods are then sold by aggressive marketing techniques that convince people that happiness is owning such and such a product. Everyone then demands higher wages to pay for these goods, and those that do not have a job have to endure the scorn of those who have, and the misery of watching their children who do not understand why they have not whilst others have. Much personal misery is born of this striving for material wealth. Also, it is becoming more and more difficult for the governing bodies to keep our beaches clean and our drinking water at an acceptable level. When the conditions become consistently bad the authorities lower the overall standard and try to convince us the new standards are an improvement.

That is like devaluing the currency. It may seem to people buying goods made in their native country that nothing has changed, but buying foreign goods becomes expensive and therefore freedom of choice is restricted. It is the same as taking a pill for a headache. When we take the pill we are merely dealing with the symptoms not solving the cause of the problem, therefore if the problem is still there, the symptoms will undoubtedly reoccur sometime in the future again. In our madness, our greed, we are polluting more and more the very substance without which we cannot live. In our efforts to force water production we have forgotten the lessons learned from the over-productions of grain which depleted the land and created the dust bowls of America and extended the desserts elsewhere. Will we be forever blind to the results of our actions until it is to late, until we annihilate ourselves?

Learning T'ai Chi teaches people to recognize clearly what they are doing and also how their actions influence others and the environment they live in. By being aware of, and seeing the results of, their actions they can, when these actions produce an effect that is detrimental to others or to the environment, make the adjustments necessary to restore balance. They can do this because they have learnt to see themselves for who they really are and they see clearly the effects of their actions. When things go well and they receive praise they enjoy it. When things do not work out as planned and they receive scorn and are rebuked, they suffer it. We all make mistakes, that is how we learn. This is part of the yin and yang of our own lives. If we can accept the yin as well as the yang, accept it as part of life's rich tapestry, if we can take responsibility for our own actions whether they produce a good or bad result (good or bad in our eyes that is because good and bad do not really exist, man by naming something good creates something that is bad), we can learn to live without fear, above all we can learn to live life more fully. T'ai Chi is the most health-enhancing exercise you will find, often described as moving meditation, moving being the operative word. Taoism shows us that life is action, action is relationship, whether the concern of that relationship is yourself, others, God, or all three. And in that action the relationship is ever developing, ever changing, never static. Everything in nature is always moving, interacting with everything else, never still. As we sleep, our blood still courses through our veins and our heart beats constantly, when it stops so does life. Stand still and you are still moving because the world on which you are standing is moving.

Is living a life of solitude, engrossed in prayer and meditation a holy existence? Is this the ultimate praise to the supreme spirit? I do not believe so, I believe that the Tao/God gave us life so that we can experience relationships and learn that to serve others is to praise the Lord and do his work. Sitting alone for hours, days and sometimes years in payer and meditation seeking enlightenment I believe is selfish. Who is to benefit except the seeker? Where is the service to anyone other than the self? Surely this only bolsters the ego and makes the seeker feel superior, intellectually.

T'ai Chi teaches people how to recognize themselves for who they are and how to react to others without increasing conflict. T'ai Chi can be practised alone and also with others, and each kind of practice will teach the participant many things, not only about themselves but also about the nature of others. There is a time to be by yourself and there is a time to be with others. How much time you spend on each is a matter of personal choice. Spend too much time on either one and disharmony within yourself will be the result, unhappiness will follow, and even illness in extreme cases. To be able to put yourself in touch with your true nature, so you can constantly keep the balance right, is to expand your potential as a human being. Taking time to place yourself in touch with your inner self will make you a more productive human being, temporally as well as spiritually.

T'ai Chi is as perennial as the Sun and the Moon. The Lee family style that I practise incorporates the Yin and Yang, the two composite factors inherent in all living things, and just as the Earth needs the sun and the moon, the light and the dark, so too do the people of the world need the principles of T'ai Chi and the lessons they teach. These lessons can help us to expand our potential as individuals and also teach us to work together for the good of humanity. T'ai Chi, like the Sun, the Moon and the Earth on which we live, is a gift, and I for one am extremely grateful for it. Like life itself, it is there to be enjoyed, for the meaning of life is living it, and the beauty of T'ai Chi is in the practice of this wonderful art.

Together we can

All true knowledge is both in the large and small, the interior and the exterior. Learn to listen to others, even the ignorant, because all have their story to tell. Each of us leads a different life path and has learnt things that are of use to others. Each of us has a unique perspective that is cultivated from our own unique individual life. This knowledge should be used to help others whenever we can. By serving others in this way we serve the Tao (God).

> > > > > >   Flow of river   > > > > > >

man looking from this direction >   < man looking from this direction

The man looking right along the river will see it as flowing away from him and a man looking left along the river will see it as flowing towards him. Without any other knowledge, each would tell a different story of the river's flow, each would be blind to the other's perspective. Everything has two parts to it to conform to the yin and yang - left, right - up, down - male, female - night, day - moving away, moving towards. An understanding of the one (essence) is reached by understanding its two composite parts which are in turn the two composite factors of everything in existence. Therefore we should not judge others opinions too harshly but listen to their story, for they have led a different path to us and may have something useful to offer. It would be a shame to miss it because we were too blinkered to see any other perspective but our own.

All rivers flow into the sea. Each finger is separate in its own right yet each combines with the others to complete the hand. Flowers make a garden. Many ants make up a nest. Many leaves are formed on a tree but these leaves cannot exist without the trunk with its roots firmly fixed in the earth. Without nourishment through the roots, the tree and therefore all those leaves will perish. The Taoist Arts of T'AI CHI - FENG SHOU - MASSAGE are themselves like the fingers of the hand, they are all separate in their own right, yet part of the hand. The fingers are part of the hand and the hand is part of the body. The body is like the trunk of a tree, it gives nourishment to the extremities. The tree's roots take sustenance from the earth. The cycle of nature created by the Tao/God continues and we are a part of that process too. If we cut ourselves off from our links with the spirit then we are reducing our potential for growth, we are like the leaves of a tree that receive moisture externally on the surface but none through the roots. The leaf survives but the development of the system (the tree) is severely restricted, and should this state of affairs continue then the tree will eventually die, and with it the leaves. The tree can survive without the leaves but the leaves cannot survive without the tree.

Flowers are a part of the garden. Individually they have a unique beauty and qualities of their own. A flower needs a garden to grown in to exist. When the flower dies off the garden abides. No individual or group is more important than the world, for it is our garden where we flower. If we do not care for our garden properly, then we restrict our own personal growth.

An instructor, or better still if you are fortunate enough to have one, a master, is like a taxi driver. You ask him to take you to your destination and if he accepts you as a fare, then he invites you to enter the vehicle. But the route must be chosen by the driver and you must trust his judgement, not dispute the route he takes you along. Trust seems to be sadly lacking in society today. Instead, we create more and more laws to restrict man's freedom. We no longer care for each other, but we are obsessed only with our own individual advancement. Everyone seeks to control everyone else's lives with more and more rules and regulations. I don't think the almighty intended us to be like robots, mechanically following a set of rules without any scope for individual expression.

A lot of rules nowadays are designed to protect the weak and unfortunate sections of our society such as the sick, the disabled or minority groups, and I wholeheartedly agree with this. I do think, however, that we are in danger of going too far to protect people from possible misfortune. Their are now so many rules and regulations that most of us commit some small crime at some time or other, like allowing our dog to empty its bowels in an area where this is forbidden, or dropping litter ourselves, or allowing others we are responsible for to, such as our children. Many others are required to insure themselves against accidentally breaking the law, needing such things as public liability insurance in case a member of the public should have an accident whilst on their property. Where will it end? Will we eventually have to insure ourselves against accidentally sneezing on someone, in case they catch a cold, and will those who do not carry this insurance be arrested and placed in jail?

If we care for the environment and our quality of life we do not allow our dogs to foul the pavements, we do not allow our dogs to foul playing areas which children frequent. Instead we take responsibility for our pets and their behaviour. Although I must confess I, personally, find it difficult to understand how anyone can claim to love an animal, then keep it chained up for most of the day while they are out at work, or how anyone can keep a bird locked up in a cage, isolated from its own species a prisoner for life. What crime did it commit? If we care for the environment we do not discard our rubbish in the street or countryside and we educate our children to place litter in the litter bins or take it home with them and dispose of it sensibly.

Together, we could have clean streets and countryside free from litter. Together, we could have rules and regulations that help society exist together congenially but at the same time do not restrict our freedom unnecessarily. To do this we must take responsibility for ourselves and our actions. We must care for others as equals, working within society, contributing in whatever way we can, with whatever skills we have at our disposal so that we are at the same time serving society and serving ourselves. Modern practices within organizations are of course developed to enhance the well-being of that organization, however, the material and the spiritual, the existent and the non-existent are governed by the same natural laws; break them, and chaos is inevitable; follow them, and harmony is assured.

Philosophers since Aristotle have debated the relationship between individuals and organizations. Aristotle argued that it is only by being part of an organization that human beings achieve their full potential. No discussion on motivation could fail to mention 'Abraham Maslow' and his five theories. These are set out and arranged into a 'hierarchy' with the highest theory being the most dominant. i.e. a)

a)   Basic needs

b)   Security

c)   Belonging

d)   Esteem or ego needs

e)   Self-actualization

a)   Basic needs - refers to such things as food, drink sleep that we all require for survival.

b)   Security - is provision for the future, security of employment etc.

c)   Belonging - is the need we all have to receive friendship. (To be part of the team.)

The employee must feel that his part of the job contributes in some way to his organization's achievement of its objectives. This feeling of participation is a great and popular method of motivation. Once this feeling of belonging is achieved, the workforce generates its own motivation and support for the management, which in turn will improve the organization's pubic image.

d) Esteem or Ego - The acquisition of possessions. Praise from others.

The ability to exercise influence over others. While these are Maslow's theories, Frederick Herzberg combined 'recognition and achievement' as great motivators. Both of these theories relate to performance and effort on the part of the employee. By putting these theories into practice we now accept 'responsibility' and the chance for 'advancement', two more of Herzbergs motivators.

e) Self - actualization needs - The need to feel self fulfillment. The need to be creative.

The majority of people studied by Maslow fitted into the 'five theory' Hierarchy, although there were some exceptions. There usually are exceptions in any theoretical study - nothing is totally yang or yin, each always contains at least a little of the other. In the case of creativity, which is a form of self-actualization, he found that this area depended upon the prior satisfaction of all the other needs, but many people could be extremely creative despite the lack of basic satisfaction. This will go a long way to prove that the more artistic and creatively minded a person is or becomes, the less they are motivated solely by monetary remuneration.

To ensure constant improvement in working conditions, every single person in an organization is responsible for improving and striving for improvement in all the general conditions at their place of work. These are known as the 'hygiene factors' according to Herzberg, and relate to the remuneration we receive; pay, fringe benefits, conditions, supervision and environment. It would be totally useless working in the most up to date building in the area, without incentives and confidence in the management. Ergonomics has been defined as the scientific study of the relationships between man and his working environment. It is derived from the Greek 'ergov' meaning work, and 'nomos' natural laws. It has been particularly relevant to the design of machines, tools and equipment, and can be an important factor in achieving the best results from the labour resource. The siting of workstations will be thoroughly researched before a decision is reached, some of the factors taken into account would be air pollution, lighting, noise and posture.

Douglas McGregor has two theories of motivation 'X & Y'. Both are described in terms of three similar propositions, but the great difference is, 'X' is usually the leader of all things and the 'Y' is lazy and needs to be led. In general terms the majority of the workforce can be a mixture of 'X & Y'. Does this remind you of the principles of the yin and yang at all? There will always be the leaders who can arrange methods of operations. The secret according to Douglas McGregor is organizing the others to reach their full potential.

When conflict rears its ugly head in an organizations, some of the main reasons are:-

a)   Group plotting to achieve their objectives at the expense of others.

b)   Managers refusing advice of knowledgeable staff.

c)   Imposing rules, restrictions to increase influence and importance.

Conflict is harmful to organizations. The consequences are low moral, lack of motivation, frustration, inefficiency. An organization suffering from conflict will perform badly.

A definition of personnel management is that part of management that is concerned with people at work and their relationship within the enterprise. Its aim is to bring together people who make up the organization and, with regard for both the well being of the individual and the working group, enable them to make their best contribution to its success.

The economic responsibility to make a profit cannot nowadays be considered in isolation from the wider social responsibilities that companies owe to their employees. Social responsibility is now expected from all organizations. It is accepted by most people now that a company's economic activity should not profit its owners at the expense of its employees. Channels of communication must keep pace with expansion. However, even the more enlightened people in top management do not always make the fullest use of all available channels of internal communication. Employer-employee understanding can be obtained and maintained, and this is the basis of sound management. Instruction is communicated, and information imparted from management to supervisors, from supervisors to subordinates, from instructors to trainee. This is a vital part of normal and administration functions.

The creation of employees' interest in the progress, results and policy of the business is an important part of management's function of motivation. By involving all employees in the organization's objectives the shock of technological change is lessened. Adequate and timely communication of changes on working conditions, wages and personnel lessens the shock and ensures that the change is more readily accepted by those affected.

Employees are given the opportunity for communication back to their employers. This is important in two ways. The employee is able to register any complaints with his employer or seek advice. The employer obtains information from his employees which often enables him to make decisions and/or improve methods. The feeling of self fulfillment which will result from this, will mean the employees are, to a large degree, motivating themselves. Maslow's five theories are satisfied. The workplace is a happier environment.

<u>The individual benefits from this.</u>

<u>The group (staff) benefit as a whole from this.</u>

<u>The organization benefits from this.</u>

The good sense and sensible working practices outlined above can be seen and understood by all. They have been developed after much research and study but these principles not only apply to large organizations and companies, they also apply to any relationship between two people, a group of people or a family unit. However, like all knowledge, these principles can be used for good or bad, like acupuncture that is use to relieve pain and suffering in Chinese medicine yet can also be used to cause pain, paralysis and even death in the deadly Chinese art of Kung Fu. The intention is what makes the difference. All knowledge is good but in the wrong hands bad. That is why all Kung Fu Masters pay attention to their senior students' state of mind as well as their physical abilities, and that is why so few attain this sort of knowledge.

I feel that we all need to concentrate on understanding and improving ourselves. Instead of pointing a finger at others' faults, if we all concerned ourselves with our own contribution to society, concerned ourselves with how we care for others instead of how much or how little they care for us, then the application of the techniques gleaned through past experiences can be used to enhance our relationship with others and the environment.

However, these same techniques can' if we should choose to use them so, be used to satisfied our own greed, our own ambitions and our own desires. The choice is ours, and we must each make our own choice. If we fall into the old excuse of saying 'WELL THEY DO IT SO I MAY AS WELL' or subscribe to the attitude that the most important rule is to look after No 1 to the exclusion of all else, then nothing will change. Things will carry on as they are, and any future improvements in technology, any advancements in the sciences or psychology, will do nothing to enhance the happiness and well-being of the human race. But, if more people endeavour to make a change within themselves so that knowledge is used in a more positive way, then, together we can move forwards, together we can accomplish a more harmonious relationship with our partners, our families, our neighbours, and our contemporaries in other countries.

I believe that all knowledge is given by God, received through the Tao, and was meant to enrich mankind. I also believe that if we use it for our own selfish aims, we restrict our own spiritual development and deny ourselves happiness. The supreme spirit, I believe, gave us free choice and the power of reason, so that we may eventually come to realize, that to love and care as best we can for ourselves, our fellow man, and also the animal kingdom and the environment is what he wishes for us. By constantly concerning ourselves only with our material expansion, neglecting to realize that this is but a temporal, a fleeting experience, realizing that all states of being are transitory, we can choose to expand our physical existence to the exclusion of our spiritual existence and vice versa, but either of these will produce extreme behaviour, balance is needed and each person must find their own. Life itself is ephemeral, so to increase one's spiritual wealth along with providing for one's material needs seems to me a more sensible approach to life. Speaking for myself, I know that the more I try to help others, the more I cooperate with others, working together with them towards a common objective, the more content I feel and the greater is my personal happiness. In the beginning the Tao/God created our universe and everything in it. These things, this energy, this life, is born of the supreme spirit. His beauty is manifested in all that there is, and we can only attain harmony by learning to love and care for all creation. Then and only then can we together be truly happy and content.

You

You are the most beautiful, the most unique, the most marvellous thing in all creation. Only the Supreme Spirit/God is greater than yourself. We were brought into existence by the Tao/God and as such were purity itself. However, seeking to glorify the self we cast a shadow on the reflection in the mirror, we muddy the waters so they can no longer reflect clearly the beauty of the supreme spirit.

If we could learn to look around us clearly we could see the results of our actions, but first you, like me, must endeavour to purify yourself, as I need to strip away my self image (my illusions of myself) to see the real me underneath. In the beginning God gave us clean water and air. Through ignorance we have muddied the water and polluted the air. Now is a time of awakening. We must reverse the process for our own survival. I believe our lack of spiritual values in favour of material growth is the cause of our stupidity and blindness. This is an illusion on our part, and ephemeral, flashy cars, big houses and large bank accounts must all be left behind when you depart this life on earth and enter the spiritual kingdom.

The sea is the heart of the world. The rivers are nature's life-blood. The rivers flow into the sea and are then sent out again to refresh and nourish nature of which we are a part. The sea is the origin of all life on this planet, and we depend on it for our continued existence. The heart is the source of our love for nature and our fellow men. When we pollute the sea we pollute ourselves. When we fill our hearts with hate instead of love we fill our minds with thoughts that lead to ambition, desire and greed, and from this many illnesses are born that attack the physical body and cause suffering. By this process we deny ourselves life.

We let fear rule our lives most of the time. Often we fear to put forward our views, we fear to stand up to others for fear of not conforming. Instead we put up a front, a mask. We elude our true selves and put up a front that smacks of strength, our own personal illusion of a lack of weakness. This is fear. We hide in it and it creates conflict. Others try to please everyone, agree with everyone, conform to the accepted view for fear of seeming different, afraid to be an individual.

To give up control, to follow the Tao, to allow God to work through you, to be devoid of self-oriented ambitions and desires, to give up the greedy collection of material wealth, to deny the self and work for the good of others, this is true courage. Those who have attained this state live without fear, protected by the Tao. As your Mother did when you were a child, the Tao will nurture you as you have never been nurtured before. True Taoists seek to attain this state of non-existence, where their every action is taken by the Tao itself, in this state of being one's every action is the action of the Tao/God, and as such can never be anything else but completely appropriate. When the self (the illusory self that is the one we create ourselves) has being wiped away so the mirror reflects truly. When the pollution has been cast out of the water so that it is pure and sparkling again, then we can be as we were truly meant to be, a unique expression of the Tao/God like no other being, a beautiful, a most marvellous thing, a joy to behold.

Again, we can learn much by watching nature. Everything in nature accepts with complete compliance, complete obedience to the way of things/the Tao. If it rains or it is windy, or if there is a storm, the plants, the trees, the animals, the fishes and birds do not complain. All in nature accepts easily and learns quickly. If there is no food or water, animals move on to new pastures, they soon learn that to stay is to perish. They know they must have food and water to survive. As human beings, because we have the power of reason, often we try to make things happen, and are consequently blinded by our desires to the way things are.

Suppose we know we have a day off work the following day and make plans to play tennis or indulge in some other outdoor activity. The next day, because when we get up to find it is raining, many of us spend the day sulking because we cannot do what we want, so we mope about and spoil our day off, which should have been relaxing. If we could have accepted the way things were without any bitterness we could have changed our plans and still had an enjoyable and relaxing day.

Weather technology makes it possible to predict weather trends, so we know what to expect, but we cannot change it. We must learn to accept it, as the farmer has to learn to plough, sow and harvest when the weather is suitable. The farmer must work with nature despite having modern machinery. If he were foolish enough to do his work in the wrong seasons or without the right weather conditions the fruits of his labours would be poor. Farmers have learnt these lessons from mistakes made in the past, they know even with machinery that will do the work of many men and increase productions manifold, they must still work with nature. The way of nature (The Tao) can be followed but it cannot be controlled. Again I am reminded that we should endeavour to:

Have the courage to change the things that ought to be changed.

The humility to accept the things that cannot be changed.

And the WISDOM to know the difference.

We have the power of reason given to us by God, and of course we should use it to benefit ourselves to make life more comfortable and harmonious, but we should realize that we cannot create anything, we can only take what the Lord gave us and do with it what we will. We can rearrange things and develop our minds in the process but we can never create anything, creation is the reserved occupation of our maker.

I have recently returned from a short holiday in Scotland with Gisela and our children. We all had a marvellous time together. For me the most enthralling experience was sitting by the river watching the salmon jumping. We found a place where the river narrowed to flow between the rocks. Here, the river of forty perhaps forty-five feet in width converged to flow between the rocks which were roughly six feet apart. At this point there was a waterfall of some five or six feet in height. The water thundered through the gap in the rocks and down the waterfall, churning its way through the ensuing gorge of grey rocks which, wet with spray, looked almost black. There we all sat, the four of us watching. At first one or the other of us would shout 'LOOK AT THAT', 'WOW!', or 'DID YOU SEE THAT ONE?', as a salmon leaped out of the water trying to ascend the waterfall. And we all sometimes cringed and uttered an 'oh' or 'ouch' as one of the fish was hurled against the rocks and then disappeared back into the churning foam. After our initial excitement and astonishment at seeing these beautiful fish making their way up the river, we became quiet - stunned into silence - the sheer tenacity of the salmon as they propelled themselves through the raging waters to leap again and again at the waterfall left us spellbound. We stayed a little more than an hour until the light began to fade and a chill entered the air, then off we went back to the car eager to get back to our chalet and have some food. We were ravenous. On the journey back to the chalet Gisela said she would like to return to the river another day and paint. Art being a hobby she enjoys, she had brought her paints along with her on the holiday. We talked with the children about it and all agreed it would be great to bring a picnic and spend a whole day by the river.

The next two days were dull and cloudy so we went elsewhere, however, the third day was bright and sunny in the morning and the weather forecast was promising (I know, but they are right sometimes) so off we went to the river again. Gisela settled down to paint while the children and I went for a little walk along the river, exploring. We had a great time climbing over the rocks. The children being brought up in the city were at first apprehensive and nervous as they scrambled about the riverbank and over the rocks, but they soon gathered confidence and thoroughly enjoyed themselves. I had a great time too. I like nothing better than being beside a swift flowing river. After a couple of hours, a little weary and a little peckish, we made our way back to where we left Gisela painting. We had seen some people fishing and the children asked if they might be allowed to fish.

Although I used to go fishing and found it very relaxing and therapeutic, I gave up the sport many years ago. I went fresh-water fishing, which is generally termed angling. Anglers do not eat the fish they catch but return them to the water. However, after having practised the Taoist Arts for a year or two, I found the standard excuse used by fishermen when accused of cruelty to the fish, that they are all cold blooded and therefore feel no pain and are returned to the water unharmed, no longer plausible. For, even if it is true that the fish do not feel any pain from the sharp point of the hook which pierces their flesh, I am sure that suddenly being jerked sharply whilst taking a bite of food, then being dragged along at high speed, wrenched out of your environment and man-handled, then thrown back, must be akin to being plucked off this earth by spacemen from another planet, examined, physically poked and prodded about, then being put back roughly where you were taken from. I have never had such an experience but if I had, I am sure it would have been a bit of a shock and taken at least a little while to get over and recover from.

So I have an ethical problem. I no longer believe in fishing for sport. Should I allow the children to fish or should I forbid it, giving them the benefit of my experience and expressing the opinion that to fish purely for pleasure is barbaric? I pondered this for a moment or two and came to the conclusion that their excitement at the prospect of catching fish was a basic hunting instinct we all possess, and that to deny them the direct experience, an experience that I myself had previously participated in, would be wrong. I felt they should experience this first hand. So I set them on the task of looking for worms. First, I showed them myself that if they lifted up the bigger rocks away from the river under the trees, and were quick about it, they could find worms underneath. I went off to get hooks and line, I was gone quite a while and when I returned the children had managed to collect a few worms and were sitting, talking with Gisela as she painted. It warmed my heart to see the radiant expression on Gisela's face. She had been painting for about three hours now, and she was loving it. The children jumped up at my arrival.

'Did you get the line and hooks dad?' they asked their voices filled with excitement.

'Yes, I have them here,' I said. 'But you will each need a stick to use as a fishing pole first.'

They were soon scrambling over the rocks and through the undergrowth in search of suitable branches. After one or two amusing instances when a stick of about six inches and another a foot long was held up and a call of, 'Is this one OK?' shouted to Gisela and me as we sat there watching them search, they found suitable ones and made their way back to us. Gisela and I looked at each other. What a wonderful time we were having, I thought to myself, me by a fast-flowing, fresh, clean, river, Gisela painting, and the children enjoying new experiences. All of us getting plenty of fresh air amongst nature, recharging our batteries. Again our eyes met. I looked deep into those big beautiful sparkling brown eyes, so full of life.

We smiled at each other. then I helped the children rig up their makeshift rods. We went to fish for minnows in a pool a few yards downstream of Gisela. who was not too happy about the children fishing. I felt, however, that as they were so eager to catch fish - minnows are only about three or four inches long, and of course once caught are immediately put back again - it should be allowed, she reluctantly agreed. The children were very excited and very impatient to catch a fish. And we all did catch a fish or two, yes even me, for I decided to fish also to show them how to do it. And what better way to teach than by example? I had to show them how to bait the hook and take the hook out of the fish once caught. It started to get dark again, so we packed up and went back to our chalet. Gisela was thrilled with her painting and I was impressed too. She said she would like to try to paint the same scene again, and as the children were now hooked on fishing we decided to return the next day.

The following day we arrived at the same spot and Gisela settled down on the same rock to paint while the children and I, fishing tackle in hand, roamed the water's edge looking for minnows. We soon found some and dropped in our lines with baited hooks to fish. Leanne my daughter was quite happy to bait her own hook, but Taio preferred me to do it for him. He was not to keen on putting a hook through the worm, and they both asked me to take the hook out of the fish when they caught one, although Leanne did try at first but was afraid of hurting the fish. I started to fish myself but was not interested really. I watched them closely. Taio had his bait nibbled off and asked me to bait his hook again for him. I told him it was time he did it for himself, and although he did not like that idea too much, the desire to catch fish was greater. So, tentatively, and with a look of disdain on his face he forced himself to complete the task. Yes, I thought, now is the time to leave them to it. I have taught them all they need to know. It's time for them to go it alone.

'I am going up river to the waterfall to watch the salmon jumping,' I said, 'Are you coming or are you going to carry on fishing?'

They both agreed they wanted to stay and fish, but they wanted me to stop to take the fish off the hook for them. I explained that if they wished to learn to fish they must learn everything themselves and that included taking the fish off the hook. With that I left them to it. I told Gisela where I was going as I passed her and that the children wished to carry on fishing so I had left them at the pool, which she could see from where she was. I also told her they were going to have to take the hooks out of any fish they caught, which I had up until now been doing for them. I looked at her painting. I was very impressed, as I have little artistic talent myself. I had intended to join a class to learn, but writing this book became more important to me. We cannot do everything at once, can we? Perhaps some day I will find the time.

To get to the spot I liked by the waterfall I had to climb down a steep bank and jump across about six foot of water to reach the rocks that gave the best view. Most people followed a path on the other side of the river, which was a little easier to negotiate but provided a poorer view of the waterfall and the run up to it. I settled down on the rocks to watch, full of excitement. Waiting to see these beautiful fish I began to feel impatient. Immediately, my eyes started to look up and down the river, searching the swirling waters for signs of a salmon. Quickly, I focused my eyes this way then that way, afraid that I might miss a chance to see a salmon jump, unable to relax and take an overall view. Then I pulled myself together. Oh yes, how easy it is to let the brain take control.

As soon as it gets the chance to have a rest and just be, it panics. Afraid to be still, the brain analyses, produces thoughts born of ambition and desires. I came to see salmon jumping and the brain says I must be successful. We live in a world full of competition, where one is supposed to make things happen. And again I had forgotten, forgotten nature is governed by the Tao (The Way). The Tao, the way of nature, can be interfered with, but it cannot be controlled by man, superior brain or not. When it comes to understanding nature we know very little indeed.

So I composed myself and just looked and listened, emptied my mind of ambition and desire, let expectations fade away and just sat there watching the water. Watched it converge into the gap between the rocks picking up speed as it did so, then watched as it roared down the waterfall and turned into a raging, swirling, churning mass of foam which hurtled through the rocky gorge at tremendous speed, just watched the water and listened to its sounds. And then it happened. Out of the water came a salmon. It seemed to hover for a second in mid air - in that instant time stopped - I creased to exist - the fish, the water, the rocks, somehow we were all one, and like that tenacious salmon leaping for all it was worth up the waterfall, everything was filled with an exuberance, everything was vibrant, and then as the salmon entered the water again and was gone. That interconnectedness was gone also. As quickly as it appeared, it disappeared. I had returned. I was me again, separate once more, and my brain produced thoughts again. But I was not the same. I was left with a feeling of exhilaration and an admiration for those gritty, determined, resolute creatures. Their struggle up river is not an easy one. It is fraught with danger and some die in the attempt. Why then do they endure this struggle time and time again? Why do they suffer these difficulties and risk their lives? They do it to lay their eggs up river where they will have a better chance of survival, where predators are fewer than further downstream or in the sea, a better chance for their offspring to grow big enough and strong enough to survive on their own. As I watched the torrential water force its way through the gorge between the rocks I marvelled at the physical prowess, the sheer power, the single-minded determination of these valiant fish swimming against the flow, following the path laid down for them by nature, the Tao. These magnificent aquatic creatures endure all this to ensure the survival of their species. And they do it with a zest, a relentlessness, that we humans cannot match. On the contrary, we seem to be only interested in what we can get for ourselves, now, without much concern for the future of our species. The lack of spiritual values in our lives leads us to think only of material comfort. So we grow fat and soft and have no interest in the welfare of our fellow man and the future of our children. We take too much and give too little.

I was reminded of my Master again, who, when faced with difficulties, shows the same courageous persistence as the salmon until the difficulties are surmounted or pass away. His only concern is the continuation, the survival, of the Taoist Arts he inherited. Suddenly, a phrase he uses when some person or other asks him why he does not delegate a menial task such as wiping a table or picking up bits off the floor in the training room came to mind, the phrase: 'I WAS BORN TO SERVE."

I continued to watch and listen. Some might call it meditation. And as I sat, I slipped in and out of that state I have come to know, where everything becomes one and there is a peace and tranquillity that cannot be described in words. I saw many salmon leap, on occasions two at a time. Sometimes they where thrown back against the rocks so hard I felt they must surely be knocked senseless, but no, time and again they came, time and again they leaped. There was no turning back here, no quitting. In this game of life survival was the prize, the continuation of life, and the participants in this game were at the same time the players, the stakes and the prize itself. Once over the waterfall and through the rapids into the next pool, they could rest and regain their strength before continuing to their destination. Just as we humans, if we wish to work at maximum efficiency, need to take periodic rests and sometime a longer rest or a holiday such as I was enjoying, to recuperate. I made a mental note to try and emulate the tenacity, the resolution and courageous persistence of the salmon and learn to balance this with adequate periods of rest.

As I sat there on the rocks, other people passed on the other side of the river. Some stopped to watch the waterfall. Many of them looked for a few seconds, and then were on their way, unaware of the thrilling spectacle awaiting them. If only they had the time to watch awhile, if only they were not so busy. Yet others stopped and asked if I had seen any fish, and when I told them I had seen many, they watched for a minute or two and then seemed to lose patience and continued on their way.

Often, caught in our eagerness to experience more, we must be constantly on the move amassing things, goods, memories, to add to our collection. Moving around quickly, taking what is available before it disappears and the chance is lost, this is the way of the world. And of course, as this is where we live, this behaviour has its place. But there is no rest in it, and holidays are for recharging our batteries, so we can build up our energy levels, as the salmon rests in the pools and gathers energy ready for the next rapid or waterfall. For good health and a long life we must endeavour to get the balance right too. As the salmon rest in the pools - calm waters - where not much effort is required and living is easy, we too must learn to rest and recover - to be still - and see what is happening, watch life go by without doing anything, just watch listen and learn. I believe if we can learn to do this, we will be able to see better the way we should proceed, and we will, certainly, after having rested awhile, have a greater supply of energy to carry us forwards. I turned my attention back to the swirling, thrashing river, strangely somehow its relentless roaring movement made it easy for me to be still.

Time passed as I sat there, an enthralled spectator of one of nature's spectacular displays. On the other side of the river, out of the trees onto the rocks, came a middle-aged man followed by a young boy of around seven or eight years old. The man watched the boy climb over the rocks closer to the river, ever watchful ever ready to help. Their view of the waterfall, and the gorge it ran into, was restricted by the rocks they stood on, which overhung the river. The man asked if I had seen any fish and I replied that I had seen lots of them trying to jump the waterfall. He spoke softly to the boy. His words were drowned by the roar of the water, but there was a sparkle in his eyes as he spoke. The boy looked at the man as he spoke, then turned and stood watching the water, and I could see and feel his excitement. The man stood behind the boy, his hands resting on the boy's shoulders in a manner that was both affectionate and protective. One or two fish jumped, but neither the man nor the boy saw them, for the overhanging rocks severely restricted their view. I glanced back upstream, at the head of the waterfall on their side of the river was a large flat rock, which afforded a much better view of the run up to the waterfall. So, shouting to make myself heard above the thundering river, I conveyed the information to them. The man smiled and thanked me, then he and the boy, very carefully, clambered over the rocks to the big flat rock - for it was dangerous here, if any of us fell into those raging waters, it was doubtful we would survive. They sat down on the rock near the water's edge, the boy in front of the man, and again the man rested his hands on the boy's shoulders. They both stared eagerly at the river. They sat there patiently, two different generations of the same species, watching and listening to nature together. The man teaching the boy about nature and its beauty. A salmon jumped and the look of startled amazement on the boy's face was a sight I will remember for a long time, for I was watching them now. It was good to see others appreciating the beauty of nature. We sat there a long time together. We were on opposite sides of the river, but there was a bond between us, a bond of love for nature. We spoke now and then about the salmon and their leaps and expressed our surprise and wonder at their ability to forge through those churning pounding waters along the gorge, and then still find the strength to leap out of the water, over the waterfall and into the torrent that swirled towards it. These spirited, glorious fish showed such a tenacity for life, that it held us spellbound. We sat there, just looking, listening and learning ,and I was reminded again that in the great scheme of things, we as individuals, do not matter too much. However, if we can be of service in some way to our fellow man, if we can serve as the salmon serves, endures, to ensure the survival of the species then as an individual serving the whole we can make a useful contribution to society. For I have found that the more I give of myself to others, the more the Tao gives back to me. However, when, as I sometimes do, I give with expectations of reward or praise I am always, always, disappointed and therefore reminded of my trespass. The man and boy stood up, and as they left that place we waved goodbye to each other and smiled as we did so. I sat pondering for a little longer, then I too got up and made my way back to Gisela and the children.

They saw me approaching as I scrambled over the rocks towards them. They were all chatting away to each other and Gisela had completed her painting, which, as I looked at it, seemed to me a great improvement on the previous day,s work. Her idea of painting the same scene again had been an excellent idea. I admired the picture, and Gisela said that she was very pleased with the result. We all gave each other a hug and I asked the children if they had become tired of fishing for the day. They explained that they had caught a fish and had found it difficult getting the hook out and had had to call to Gisela to come and help them. Gisela had managed to get the hook out but the fish was bleeding a little when they returned it to the water and this dampened their enthusiasm for fishing for the time being at least. So we packed up and went off to base. The fresh air had made us all very hungry. An excellent day, I thought. We have all learnt much about each other and nature, the children from their fishing, and Gisela from her painting, and I from my observations. And together from our relationship with each other.

Much later, when the children had gone to bed, I thought of the salmon and its understanding of its world, the waters of the rivers and sea. It knows nothing of the world above the surface of the water, apart from when, for a few fleeting moments, it leaps clear. It seemed to me akin to the few fleeting moments when, lost in meditation, I cease to exist as a separate individual and somehow blend in with the rest of nature. At these times, the sky, land, water, trees and even the atmosphere, the air, become united in a single entity. Is this then, like the salmon's leap, my leap, my glimpse of a greater reality? A glimpse beyond the confines of the physical world we live in, out of our everyday environment. As the salmon do, I leap into a world beyond my comprehension, where I can only look and listen. A world where the logical, analytical thought of the physical world, produced as it is in man's brains, is no longer relevant. Is the logical, analytical thought merely a collection of memories of past experiences, which we draw on to guide us when dealing with the physical domain in which we exist?

The science of astronomy suggests that there are many universes beyond ours, and that on some of those, according to the laws of probability, life will exist. Within our world there are other's worlds, like the world of the salmon and other water creatures. Everything in nature, the soil, the rocks, the trees, the water, the very air we breathe, is composed of different particles. Our own bodies have millions upon millions of molecules which in turn compose systems for processing air, water and food. Our cardio-vascular system carries nutrients and oxygen around the body and conveys waste products and carbon dioxide out. Our blood vessels are in this world that is our body, our rivers, and the place from whence the blood is sent out, and to which it must return is the heart, just as the sea is the heart of our external world. So it would seem to me that the knowledge of the external and the knowledge of the internal, the large and the small, offer the same lessons. The two composite factors inherent in everything in existence, the Yin and Yang, which emanate from the Tao, the principles of which everything from the smallest microbe to the largest star must adhere to, apply also to every living being, including you.

You, with all these millions and millions of molecules, are a more complex organism than any mankind has ever been able to put together. Also, every one of us is unique. No two alike. Each one of us is capable of our own individual expression of the Tao. Each of us can be anything we want to be. All you have to do is work towards it, now. Forget about time restraints. These are man-made obstacles. It does not matter how long it takes to acquire the skills or attributes you seek. Once you have them at your disposal, in fact whatever you learn, no one can take that knowledge away from you. The more you learn about yourself and the world in which you live, the better teacher you will be. Yes, teacher. We are all teachers. We teach by example. By our actions in everyday life, we show the young in our community how much respect we have for others and the environment. So if we are not happy with their behaviour then we should look closely at ourselves; for we are the example they learnt from.

The more you can learn to see the path of your own life and follow it - apart from the few occasions when you may, temporarily, like the salmon, have to swim against the flow in the service of others, or, for purely survival reasons - the more harmonious, constructive and happy will be your existence. You can learn to use your skills to assist others, as your fingers help each other and make your hands more useful to you than the individual fingers, and as both hands working together, when needed, are more useful to you than each individual hand is in isolation. If as individuals we can work together for the community, the environment, our world, then in this way we will be serving God/the Tao and also increasing our spiritual wealth and ensuring the survival of our species. The world we live in will become a better place for all who dwell there, man and beast. And who can achieve this transformation? The United Nations? The EEC? The President or Prime Minister of our country? NO. You and I, together.

The small produces the large. Consider a wheel. At the centre is a small hub. From a little seed mighty oaks grow. Babies grow into adults. Our votes elect our representatives, who make important decisions on our behalf. By taking responsibility for ourselves and our actions, the significant change we make within ourselves as an individual will be an example to others. And the more people who make a change within themselves, the greater the effect on the whole. Why should we do this? For the same reason the salmon fights its way upstream to spawn. To ensure our children have a habitable, hospitable world to grow up in.

A Winter's Walk

Here I am, working on the closing chapter of my book, as nature changes from summer to winter. How apt. Nature rests itself during the winter season and then surges into life again the following spring, just as Yang things must eventually become Yin and Yin must change to Yang, summer turns to winter, and then winter back to summer again in the perpetual cycle of the seasons of the year.

So much has happened to me while I have been writing this book. My life has changed in so many ways. It was in October 1992 that I started taking a T'ai Chi class in Scarborough and met Gisela again, who has become my fiancée, and next year, God willing, will be my wife. I never thought I would marry again. I believed that my life style was such that no woman would be prepared to put up with it. In fact, about six years ago, just after my previous marriage had broken down, and I suppose I must have been looking a lonely figure, one day during the lunch break of a training weekend my Master Chee Soo looked deep into my eyes and said. 'One day you will meet someone else.'

I said, 'I think I must be destined to spend my life alone. No woman in her right mind will put up with my dedication to the arts.'

'You will find someone. You'll see,' he said.

'I think I prefer to stay on my own,' I said. 'It's less hassle.'

''But it's not natural,' he said. 'When a man and woman join together, they must always remember that they are also two separate individuals. If they can recognize this, they can be in harmony together.' Wise words from a wise man.

I love to go for little walks, sometimes with company but sometimes I need to walk alone, to look at nature, to think of what I need to do, to reflect and ponder. This was such a walk I was taking now. Autumn was turning the leaves yellow, orange and brown. The flowers were starting to die off. Soon all nature would look barren and dull. But the trees have their roots sunk firmly in the ground. The seeds and bulbs will be safe from the cold and frost of winter, safe in the soil, the flesh of Mother Earth.

The seasons which make up a year are never the same twice. No winter or summer is ever exactly like the previous one, similar but not quite the same. Nothing in nature is ever reproduced exactly. Each new occurrence is always just that, new, fresh. This is the chaos that is the Tao. It cannot be anticipated, but if one watches nature without trying to analyse or judge, in fact without any conscious thought at all, then one can start to see an order that cannot be manipulated or changed. That essence within the chaos is the principle which governs nature and all in the cosmos. This will lead to the realization that the less you do to interfere with this process the more you will accomplish, and this is non action, following the way, working with the principle, the way of harmony.

I thought of the book I had written. I felt proud of myself (are Taoists supposed to feel proud? answers on a postcard please). I had not completed the work on schedule, but I had persevered and when events had distracted me from the task, I had gone with the flow. I had bent with the wind, and then when the storm was over I had returned to the task. I had exercised discipline in myself. At the outset I had showed courage at what seemed an enormous task. To write a book, to write well in excess of 60,000 words had been a daunting prospect. I had used all the tools at my disposal. I had used mathematics to break down the large figure into a weekly total, I had set aside time to complete this, and although this goal I set myself with no previous experience was grossly over estimated, it had reduced the daunting prospect of 60,000 words to 2,400 words a week, which my logical brain could envisage as a viable proposition. I received all of the ideas expressed in this book. I was given them all. Some came from watching my students train. Many of course came from the lessons I have been taught by my Master. Some came from listening to friends and my fiancée's opinions during our discussions, for we love to talk together. Some came to me during my walks or as I observed nature, given by the Tao. And I have expressed them as best I can.

Chee Soo consented to preside over a course I had arranged in Scarborough. The students were thrilled to see him, and I was deeply honoured. He and his wife Marilyn came a few days before the course, and Gisela and I were able to show them around a little. As we sat in Gisela's house enjoying a chat and a cup of tea, my mind was numb as I listened to my Master tell me he intended to retire the following year. I found it hard to believe, especially as two days later he gave a demonstration of distance and timing skills with three senior students, all of whom were between twenty seven and thirty two years younger than him, which was breath-taking. I have never seen a more accomplished practitioner, never seen anyone who is so able a master of self defence, and at the same time expresses no aggression himself. Without a doubt, Chee Soo is definitely a unique Taoist Master, and I am extremely grateful to have been able to train with him.

A few days later, I contemplated these recent events as I stopped to rest from my walking and sat for a while to watch the sea. The tide is going out. Slowly, the tide recedes, but it will return. The Tao wills it so. What changes to my life will these new unforeseen circumstances have? Flowers and trees shed their seeds, and those that survive, bury themselves in the earth and take nourishment from and are protected by Mother Earth. There are many diverse family structures in nature. Some creatures rear their young and then send them out to fend for themselves, knowing full well that only the strong will survive and the weak will perish. I am reminded of the process my Master took me through. Like the master craftsman, he took, me, the rough piece of metal, and placed it in the fire, heated it until it glowed red hot, like the aggression and passion he raised to the surface in me, then as the master craftsman does, he tempered my body and mind, tempered my aggression and passion. His intention is to produce a fine sword. He loves his work and is always trying to improve it to make a finer tool. The sword of a master craftsman is not an implement of destruction, it is an implement of protection. Hard yet flexible, it incorporates the Yin and Yang, and in the hands of a master swordsman can keep the peace without ever been raised in battle.

This process is not a process of mass production, for while many come to the door, few are able to stand the heat and tempering treatment for long. As I sat there pondering these things, I hope my Master had time to equip me with the necessary strength of character to carry on his work. I do not have his skills but I have been given the seeds from which they grow. If I can bury myself in the Tao, I will be given the nourishment I need. I will survive,.I will prosper. I will serve.

Other creatures rear their young, and when they are old enough their children take a partner and have their own families while continuing to be a part of the larger group, a useful contributor to the extended family. I ponder the possibilities. I have no expectations, no wishes, for as they raise themselves in my thoughts I look at them, then let them pass on. I do not hang on to them, analyse them, but let them go. They live and then they die. Like the tide they come in and then they go out again. The future, my future, and yours for that matter, is in the hands of the Tao, and my predestined path will unfold with the passage of time. No amount of pushing and shoving on my part, mentally or physically, will alter anything, in fact it would only create conflict, and there is enough of that already without me adding to it.

Time passes, and I busy myself with doing my best to teach people the Taoist Arts as taught to me. It is exciting and very rewarding. Many people express their appreciation and extol the benefits of T'ai Chi and the other Taoist Arts on their health. So, as I come to the end of this, my first book, I reflect on the many changes in my life since I typed the first words. I have met a truly wonderful woman with whom to share my life. My Master who has been my mentor and teacher for so long, is drifting away like the tide, however, we will of course remain friends. Gisela and I will, with his permission, visit him and his wife Marilyn.

I have no idea where my dedication to the Taoist Arts will take me in the future, but I do know that teaching these arts is what I am meant to do. So, as my mentor and teacher sends me out into the world to fend for myself and continue his work ,I have by my side a wonderful, supportive partner. I am indeed a lucky man for the Tao nurtures me and sees to my needs. As I have expressed the understanding I have learned of Taoist philosophy, as I have given of myself, I have been given much, much more in return. So what now then, now that I have finished writing my book? A phrase used by my Master springs from nowhere into my mind: When you come to the end of everything, you must start again at the beginning.   WISE WORDS FROM A WISE MAN. Perhaps I should write another book.